Novell
GroupWise 6.5

USER'S HANDBOOK

Shawn Rogers
Richard McTague

Novell
PRESS™

Novell®

800 East 9 a 46240 USA

Novell GroupWise 6.5 User's Handbook

International Standard Book Number: 0-789-72983-0

Library of Congress Catalog Card Number: 2003102740

Printed in the United States of America

First Printing: September 2003

06 05 04 03   4 3 2 1

Trademarks

All terms mentioned in this book that are known to be trademarks or service marks have been appropriately capitalized. Sams Publishing cannot attest to the accuracy of this information. Use of a term in this book should not be regarded as affecting the validity of any trademark or service mark. Novell, GroupWise, NetWare and Novell iFolder are registered trademarks and Novell Press is a trademark and CNE is a registered service mark of Novell, Inc. in the US and other countries.

Warning and Disclaimer

Every effort has been made to make this book as complete and as accurate as possible, but no warranty or fitness is implied. The information provided is on an "as is" basis. The author(s) and the publisher shall have neither liability nor responsibility to any person or entity with respect to any loss or damages arising from the information contained in this book.

Bulk Sales

Sams Publishing offers excellent discounts on this book when ordered in quantity for bulk purchases or special sales. For more information, please contact

    U.S. Corporate and Government Sales
    1-800-382-3419
    corpsales@pearsontechgroup.com

For sales outside of the U.S., please contact

    International Sales
    1-317-428-3341
    international@pearsontechgroup.com

Acquisitions Editor
Jenny Watson

Development Editor
Emmett Dulaney

Managing Editor
Charlotte Clapp

Project Editor
Elizabeth Finney

Copy Editor
Bart Reed

Indexer
Chris Barrick

Proofreader
Katherin Bidwell

Technical Editor
Warren Wyrostek

Team Coordinator
Vanessa Evans

Page Layout
Kelly Maish
Plan-it Publishing

Contents At a Glance

Table of Contents

Welcome to Novell Press

Novell Press, the world's leading provider of networking books, is the premier source for the most timely and useful information in the networking industry. Novell Press books cover fundamental networking issues as they emerge—from today's Novell and third-party products to the concepts and strategies that will guide the industry's future. The result is a broad spectrum of titles for the benefit of those involved in networking at any level: end user, department administrator, developer, systems manager, or network architect.

Novell Press books are written by experts with the full participation of Novell's technical, managerial, and marketing staff. The books are exhaustively reviewed by Novell's own technicians and are published only on the basis of final released software, never on pre-released versions.

Novell Press at Que Publishing is an exciting partnership between two companies at the forefront of the knowledge and communications revolution. The Press is implementing an ambitious publishing program to develop new networking titles centered on the current versions of NetWare, GroupWise, ZENworks, BorderManager, and networking integration products.

Novell Press books are translated into several languages and sold throughout the world.

Darrin VandenBos
Publisher
Novell Press, Novell, Inc.

Preface

Introduction to GroupWise 6.5

Welcome to GroupWise 6.5! You have in front of you a tool to open the vast world of collaboration with your peers—within your company and with your partners, vendors, suppliers, and customers—regardless of your location.

Of course, email itself has been and continues to be a popular method of communication. GroupWise goes way beyond simple email (which it does very well) to a very effective collaboration tool, contact manager, daily planner, and document interface.

It is flexible enough to work for you at whatever level you feel comfortable with. If you just need email, fine! If you want to share a folder and build rules to automatically place all project emails in that shared folder, great! If you are a member of an Internet newsgroup and want access to those messages, excellent!

GroupWise fits the bill perfectly.

Chapter 1: Introduction to GroupWise 6.5

In this chapter we introduce you to the overall functionality of GroupWise and discuss the interface of GroupWise—the main screen—and how you navigate through it. We focus on the Windows GroupWise program (the Web browser version, called "GroupWise WebAccess," is covered in Chapter 12). Additional items covered in this chapter include starting GroupWise, a folders overview, and navigating through GroupWise. When you finish this chapter, you will understand how the interface works and how you can use it to access the "information sources" covered in subsequent chapters.

Chapter 2: What's New in GroupWise 6.5

In this chapter we look at all the new features for GroupWise 6.5. Novell put most of the development effort for this version into the client software—the program users run to access the information in GroupWise. The goal was to make it more user friendly by making it easier to do the most common tasks.

In addition, GroupWise 6.5 adds significant new features, such as the Contacts folder, Checklist folder, and Categories. GroupWise 6.5 also enhances features that already existed in earlier versions and made them easier and more powerful to use, such as filters, the Calendar, Toolbars, and significant Address Book enhancements.

Chapter 3: Messaging Fundamentals

This chapter explains how to use the "core" features of GroupWise—sending and receiving email messages. We cover the different GroupWise accounts that are possible, the different message types, and how to read, respond, forward, and delete messages. Whether you have used email for years or are just beginning with GroupWise, you'll find that this chapter makes you much more productive with the most popular message type—email messages.

Chapter 4: The GroupWise Address Book

One of the biggest areas of enhancement in GroupWise 6.5 is in the Address Book. The transformation from a simple address-lookup feature to a more powerful contact-management tool has been completed in this release of GroupWise. The traditional features, such as name completion and shared address books, are still in place, and new features, such as the Contacts folder, have been added to the Address Book. We cover each of these features in this chapter and show you how to leverage the Address Book for contact management.

Chapter 5: Message Management

The amount of information that we receive and send on a daily basis in the form of email is staggering, and it never seems to lessen. We get more and more email every day, and this chapter focuses on how to manage that influx of information. Organizing messages using the Cabinet, managing outgoing messages, and deleting messages are all covered in this chapter. This chapter also deals with how to extract information—finding the information you're looking for, using filters, printing, and archiving messages are all covered.

Chapter 6: Personal Calendaring and Task Management

In this chapter we discuss how to leverage the Calendar system within GroupWise 6.5 to effectively manage your personal time, using appointments, tasks, and reminder notes. We introduce you to the Calendar interface and walk you through creating posted appointments, tasks, and reminder notes. In addition, we show you several easy and convenient methods to manage your calendar, including rescheduling and changing Calendar entries from one type to another.

Chapter 7: Group Calendaring and Task Management

Taking personal calendaring to the next level, this chapter deals with collaborating with others using meetings, delegating tasks, and sending reminder notes to others. We show you how to monitor those invitations, how to retract or reschedule them, and how to set up recurring events. Finally, we cover additional Calendar topics, such as how to view multiple calendars at the same time and how to print a calendar using the many different printing formats built in to GroupWise 6.5.

Chapter 8: Advanced Features

This is the chapter that really sets you apart as a true GroupWise 6.5 power user. It covers the advanced features of GroupWise that allow you to use the program to its fullest potential. We cover such topics as GroupWise rules, Proxy, discussions, Junk Mail Handling, and advanced security options. You will also find configuration options for customizing the appearance of GroupWise, message notification, managing your Mailbox size, repairing your Mailbox, and other new advanced features. Finally, we cover accessing other email accounts with GroupWise, including how to import settings, email, and addresses into GroupWise.

Chapter 9: Document Management

The built-in document management system (DMS) in GroupWise 6.5 allows you to tightly integrate your information management of everyday documents, spreadsheets, and presentations into your GroupWise program. Using GroupWise DMS, you can create, open, and share your documents with other users, as well as leverage powerful features such as version control, historical access, and document security. We also show you how to import your existing documents into "document libraries" with GroupWise.

Chapter 10: Remote Access

In today's mobile society, accessing information regardless of your location is a key requirement. GroupWise offers several different options on remote access. This chapter covers using the primary Windows-based GroupWise client in Remote Mode, allowing you to work on your messages, appointments, and documents while disconnected from the network. Once you are reconnected to the network—whether it is your company's internal network or the Internet—you can synchronize your

GroupWise remote Mailbox with your Mailbox at your corporate office, sending your outgoing messages and obtaining your incoming messages. This chapter covers how to prepare GroupWise for remote access and how to use GroupWise in Remote Mode.

Chapter 11: Customizing GroupWise

Out of all the chapters in this book, you're sure to find this chapter to be the most fun because it deals with customizing GroupWise to suit your tastes. For example, if you would like the three functions you use most often as the only buttons on the Toolbar, we show you how to accomplish this. We also show you how to customize your folders, set default fonts and views for reading and sending messages, and display messages in different formats, such as discussion threads.

Chapter 12: Mobile GroupWise Access

This chapter discusses how you can access GroupWise from a number of wireless devices, including personal digital assistants (PDAs), cell phones, and other devices dedicated to messaging (such as Blackberry's RIM devices). We show how GroupWise automatically senses the device you are connecting with and formats the information appropriately.

Appendix A: GroupWise Startup Options

This appendix covers the options that allow the GroupWise client to operate in Online, Cache, or Remote Mode.

Appendix B: GroupWise Resources

This appendix provides numerous additional resources for finding more GroupWise information—sources on the Internet, within the GroupWise Help facility, and in the "Cool Solutions" community.

About the Authors

Shawn B. Rogers, Master Certified Novell Engineer (MCNE), is the author or co-author of seven previous books on Novell GroupWise. He is employed by Hewlett-Packard Company in Houston, Texas as worldwide project manager for the HP Certified Professional program. Formerly, he was a senior instructional designer for Novell Education. He has nine years' teaching and technical instructional design experience with GroupWise and other computing technologies.

Richard H. McTague is employed by Novell as a Solution Partner in Dallas, Texas for Novell Consulting. He is the co-author of six books by Novell Press for GroupWise, and he has eight years' experience in designing messaging system and certification training around GroupWise and other technologies.

Dedication

I dedicate this book to Kellie, Cameron, and Carlie.

—Shawn Rogers

I dedicate this book to Alison, Richard, Patrick, and James.

—Rick McTague

Acknowledgments

I want to thank Kellie, Cameron, and Carlie for their love and support. As with all previous books, the sacrifice to give daddy "book time" was real, and required an extra measure of patience.

Thanks, as always, to my co-author and friend, Rick McTague, who drove this project from the beginning. His competence and enthusiasm made this and all six previous projects both enjoyable and successful.

—*Shawn Rogers*

I would like to first of all thank my family, who (as they did with the previous books) gave me the time and space needed to work on this project, and whose patience and support I deeply appreciate.

And a big "shout out" goes to my good friend and co-author Shawn Rogers, whom I can always count on for timely and in-depth contributions. We easily slipped back into the routine of co-writing, and it made this project seem to go a lot faster. I really enjoy working with him and value our friendship.

—*Rick McTague*

We would like to jointly thank Jenny Watson, Emmett Dulaney, and Warren E. Wyrostek for their project coordination, editorial assistance, and technical assistance, respectively. It has been a sincere pleasure to work with such an efficient and professional group of individuals.

We Want to Hear from You!

As the reader of this book, *you* are our most important critic and commentator. We value your opinion and want to know what we're doing right, what we could do better, what areas you'd like to see us publish in, and any other words of wisdom you're willing to pass our way.

You can email or write me directly to let me know what you did or didn't like about this book—as well as what we can do to make our books stronger.

Please note that I cannot help you with technical problems related to the topic of this book, and that due to the high volume of mail I receive, I might not be able to reply to every message.

When you write, please be sure to include this book's title and author as well as your name and phone or email address. I will carefully review your comments and share them with the author and editors who worked on the book.

E-mail: feedback@novellpress.com

Mail: Mark Taber
            Associate Publisher
            Que Publishing/Novell Press
            800 East 96th Street
            Indianapolis, IN 46240 USA

Reader Services

For more information about this book or others from Novell Press or Que Publishing, visit our Web site at **www.quepublishing.com**. Type the ISBN (excluding hyphens) or the title of the book in the Search box to find the book you're looking for.

Introduction to GroupWise 6.5

In this chapter you'll learn about the GroupWise 6.5 client interface. The GroupWise client is the software you use to interact with a GroupWise system or another type of email system, and an interface is the user's view of a program (it's what you, the user, interact with to control the program). This chapter briefly introduces you to the main parts of the GroupWise client interface.

Different Versions of GroupWise

The GroupWise client is supported on Microsoft Windows 95, Windows 98, Windows NT, Windows 2000, Windows Me, and Windows XP. GroupWise also has a special WebAccess client that can be used through any of the popular Internet-browsing programs, such as Microsoft Internet Explorer and Netscape Navigator. Using the WebAccess client, you access your GroupWise account from other operating systems that support Web browsing, such as Macintosh and Unix. You can also use a personal digital assistant (PDA) or a wireless telephone to access information in a GroupWise system. No matter which one you use to access GroupWise, each client or device has basically the same features, but the way you use those features can vary depending on the capabilities of the environment.

In this book we emphasize the GroupWise client for the Microsoft Windows platform. We also devote several pages to the GroupWise WebAccess client. These are the two most commonly used means of accessing your GroupWise account.

No matter which method you use to interact with GroupWise, all GroupWise users deal with common message formats. It does not matter which version of the client you use to create a message, and it doesn't matter which version of the client the recipient uses to read the message. (In fact, if you are communicating through the Internet with users outside of your company's GroupWise installation, those users are very likely using completely different email systems.) The point is that you can send messages to people using different email systems, different computing platforms, and different email interfaces without knowing anything about those other systems, platforms, or interfaces.

Starting GroupWise

The GroupWise program can be launched in different ways. The most common is to simply double-click the GroupWise icon located on your Windows desktop. If the icon is not available on your desktop, you would click Start, Programs, Novell GroupWise, GroupWise. Normally, when you perform one of these actions, GroupWise simply opens up your mailbox.

NOTE This book was written based on a GroupWise 6.5 default client installation running on Windows 2000 Professional. If you are running a different version of Windows, you might use a slightly different procedure to launch GroupWise.

However, the very first time you run GroupWise, you might see the GroupWise Startup screen. You use this screen to provide GroupWise with your user ID, post office information, and TCP/IP settings. Don't panic if you encounter this screen—your system administrator can give you all the necessary information. We assume for the rest of the chapter that you don't need to deal with the Startup screen.

TIP Appendix A, "GroupWise Startup Options," provides more information about the Startup screen.

The Main GroupWise Screen

When you open the GroupWise 6.5 client for the first time, the screen shown in Figure 1.1 appears automatically. You access all the GroupWise features from this screen. We call this part of the interface the *main*

GroupWise screen. From the main GroupWise screen, you access your
incoming messages, outgoing messages, deleted messages, documents
stored in a GroupWise library, and any items on your calendar. You can
also access other email accounts you might happen to use. (We explain
how to set all this up in Chapter 8, "Advanced Features.") The
GroupWise interface looks similar to other Windows applications—in
particular, it bears close resemblance to Windows Explorer, and it functions in much the same way.

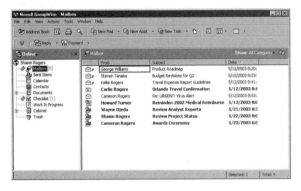

FIGURE 1.1
The GroupWise interface provides access to all GroupWise features.

TIP You can open multiple GroupWise windows and customize each one with a different view of your GroupWise information.

As you can see in Figure 1.1, the main screen has five principal areas:

▶ **Menu**—The GroupWise options menu, under the title bar

▶ **Toolbar**—Buttons that provide shortcuts to commonly used menu
options

▶ **Folders List**—The list of folder icons where your messages are
organized

▶ **Items Area**—The area where messages are stored

▶ **Summary**—An indicator that shows the number of selected and
total messages in the highlighted folder

These interface elements comprise the basic control elements of the main
GroupWise screen and allow you to interact with the program efficiently.

The Folders List and Items Area

The two most useful parts of the main GroupWise screen are the Folders List and the Items Area. The Folders List contains a hierarchical structure of the folders that are used to organize and hold messages and documents. The Items Area displays the individual messages that are located in the selected folder. The Folders List and Items Area are linked to each other. To view the items in a folder, simply select the folder in the Folders List on the left; the items in that folder then display in the Items Area on the right.

Nine folders appear automatically in the main GroupWise screen. In Chapter 5, "Message Management," you learn how to adjust the settings for these folders and how to create new folders for storing your messages. Table 1.1 lists the nine system-generated default folders and describes their functions:

TABLE 1.1   Default GroupWise Folders

FOLDER NAME	DESCRIPTION
Mailbox	Displays the messages you have received. (Mailbox management is explained in Chapter 5.)
Sent Items	Displays the messages you have sent to other email recipients and allows you to obtain the status of the messages and perform other actions on those messages.
Calendar	Displays your calendar, which stores information about your appointments, notes, and tasks. (Calendar management is explained in Chapter 6, "Personal Calendaring and Task Management.")
Contacts	Displays your personal contacts. These are contacts that are in your Frequent Contacts address book. (The Address Book is explained in Chapter 4, "The Address Book and the Address Selector.")
Documents	Contains subfolders that display the documents you have authored and the documents in your default library. (Document management is explained in Chapter 9, "Document Management.")

TABLE 1.1   Continued

FOLDER NAME	DESCRIPTION
Checklist	Displays a list of items that require an action of some type. This can be used for task management. (Task Management is discussed in Chapter 7, "Group Calendaring and Task Management.")
Work In Progress	Keeps drafts of unsent messages until you're ready to send them.
Cabinet	Displays the messages you have filed for storage. (Message management is explained in Chapter 5.)
Trash	Displays the items you have deleted.

The following subsections describe each of the default system folders in more detail.

Mailbox

When you want to see your new messages, you must open the Mailbox folder. When you receive a new message, an unopened envelope icon displays next to the Mailbox folder. The number of unopened messages in your mailbox also displays to the right of the Mailbox folder.

You open the Mailbox folder simply by clicking it. You will see a list of your opened and unopened messages in the Items Area, as shown earlier in Figure 1.1. To read a message, double-click the message line. The message will open in a new window.

Sent Items

The Sent Items folder is your outbox. This folder is used to manage the messages you have sent, and it lets you perform these three useful tasks:

▶ View the status of the messages you have sent

▶ Resend messages

▶ Retract messages you have sent (provided that the messages have not been opened yet)

Figure 1.2 shows the Sent Items folder. The first time you double-click an item in the Sent Items folder, a dialog box appears asking you what you want the double-click action to perform in the future. You have the choice of either having the message open or having the status information appear. This dialog box only displays the first time you double-click a sent item. Your choice in this dialog box becomes your default action. (You can change this option later by clicking Tools, Options, Environment.)

FIGURE 1.2
The Sent Items folder allows you to access and manage messages you have sent.

When you view the status information of a message, you can see detailed information about what has happened to the message since you sent it; you can see information such as when the message was delivered, opened, deleted, completed (if the message was a task), forwarded, accepted, or declined (if the message was an appointment or a task).

The Sent Items folder is a special type of folder known as a *query folder*. Folders are explained in more detail in Chapter 5.

From the Sent Items folder, you can resend messages that need to be updated, modified, or sent to additional recipients. To resend a message, select the Resend option from the Actions menu. When you edit and resend a message, you can retract the original message as long as the recipient has not opened it yet.

To retract a message, highlight the message in the Sent Items screen and press the Delete key. Next, select either Recipient's Mailbox or All Mailboxes. (Selecting the My Mailbox feature will not retract the message but instead delete it from your Sent Items folder.) Deleting from the recipient's mailbox will retract the message and leave a copy of the message in your Sent Items folder. Deleting from all mailboxes retracts the message and also deletes the message from your Sent Items folder.

TIP You can only retract messages that have not been opened by the recipient.

Calendar

The Calendar feature lets you create, view, and manage your appointments, tasks, and notes. These Calendar items can be personal items (for example, a personal note to yourself), or they can be group items (for example, a meeting request). Figure 1.3 shows the Calendar.

Appointments   Notes

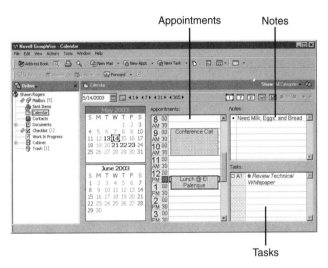

Tasks

FIGURE 1.3
The Calendar provides access to your appointments, tasks, and notes.

NOTE Chapters 6 and 7 explain personal and group calendaring in more detail.

You can view your Calendar items in the Items Area by clicking the Calendar folder. To view the Calendar as its own window, click Window and choose Calendar. Then select the Calendar view you want to see, such as Week. You can also click the Calendar button on the Toolbar.

Documents

GroupWise can be used as a full-featured document-management system. The Documents folder displays references to documents that have been

stored in a GroupWise library. These might be documents you have created or documents created by other individuals. GroupWise document
management is explained in Chapter 9.

Checklist

The Checklist folder is used to keep track of items requiring an action. It
displays items in your personal task list. (The first time you open the
Checklist folder, you will see an information screen that gives you an
overview of this folder, which goes away after you place a task into the
folder.) This includes both tasks you have created yourself and tasks
assigned to you by others. Figure 1.4 shows the Checklist. (Tasks are
explained in more detail in Chapters 6 and 7.)

A task is something that requires an action on your part, such as following up on an email message or returning a telephone call. Each task has a
start date and a due date. Overdue tasks are carried forward in the
Calendar views.

If you send a task item to someone else, and that person accepts the task,
you can track its status by opening the task from the Sent Items folder.

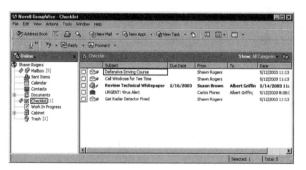

FIGURE 1.4
The Checklist folder allows you to manage your tasks.

Work In Progress

You can use the Work In Progress folder to store drafts of messages that
have not been sent, as shown in Figure 1.5. For example, if you begin
writing a message and you run out of time to complete it or you need to
obtain additional information, you can save a draft of the message in the

Work In Progress folder. Later, you can retrieve the message from this folder, complete it, and send the message along to the recipients.

The Work In Progress folder is also useful for storing drafts of documents if you are using the document-management features of GroupWise.

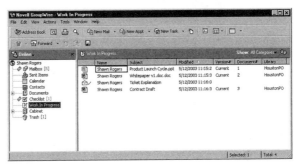

FIGURE 1.5
Work In Progress allows you to save drafts of messages for later completion.

Cabinet

The Cabinet contains additional folders used to organize your messages. Figure 1.6 shows an example of the Cabinet. Use this folder to organize messages in the same way you use the directory and subdirectory structure on your computer to organize files. You can place messages that pertain to the same project in a folder, nest folders inside other folders, and link messages to multiple folders. (Chapter 5 explains more about folders and how to manage your messages.)

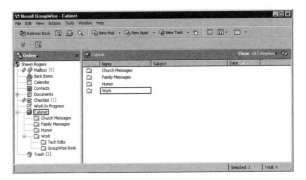

FIGURE 1.6
The GroupWise Cabinet lets you organize and manage your messages.

Trash

When you delete a message from anywhere in GroupWise, the message goes into the Trash. Later, if you need to undelete the message, you can retrieve it from the Trash, provided that the Trash has not been emptied. (Chapter 5 discusses managing messages in the Trash folder.)

To view the messages in the Trash, simply click the Trash folder. Figure 1.7 shows how the Trash folder looks when it is open. Messages do not remain in the Trash forever. They stay there for a specified period of time and then they are emptied from the Trash. When a message is emptied from the Trash, it is completely deleted from your GroupWise mailbox and you cannot retrieve it again. (Your GroupWise system administrator might be able to recover items that have been deleted from the Trash. Contact your system administrator if a situation arises in which you absolutely must retrieve items that have been deleted from the Trash.) Messages are automatically emptied from the Trash after 7 days. However, you can adjust this number to choose the number of days you want deleted messages to stay in the Trash before they are automatically emptied. (Chapter 11, "Customizing GroupWise," explains how to set this option.)

In some GroupWise configurations, you might be prompted to confirm a final deletion of an item that has not yet been backed up by the GroupWise system. If a document has not been backed up by the GroupWise system, it cannot be restored at a later date. This is a special protection mechanism known as a *smart purge*, which may or may not be enabled by your GroupWise system administrator. If you receive this prompt, make sure the message is not needed again for any reason.

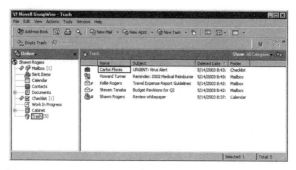

FIGURE 1.7
The Trash stores your deleted messages.

Navigating Within GroupWise

As you work with GroupWise, you will discover that there are many different ways to accomplish individual tasks. In this book we try to consistently explain the easiest steps to follow. Like other Windows-based applications, the GroupWise client contains pull-down menus, scrollbars, and minimize, maximize, and close buttons consistent with accepted Windows conventions.

You can click any corner of the GroupWise interface and drag it to a new position on the screen to resize the main GroupWise screen. You can also click and drag the dividing bar between different panes of the main screen to resize the panes. Likewise, you can click and drag messages from the Items Area to the folders in the Cabinet or other system folders.

In many situations, you can use alternative methods to execute the menu commands. For example, to send a mail message, you can click File, New, Mail. Alternatively, you can simply click the New Mail button on the Toolbar, or you can press Ctrl+M.

Several GroupWise features can help you navigate within GroupWise more quickly and efficiently. These features include the Toolbar, keystroke shortcuts, QuickMenus, and QuickViewer.

The Toolbar

The Toolbar, shown in Figure 1.8, is the row of buttons under the menu bar in the main GroupWise screen. You can use the buttons on the Toolbar as shortcuts to activate options that otherwise appear under the pull-down menus. Using the Toolbar, you can quickly access the GroupWise features you use most often. Editing functions (such as Cut, Copy, and Paste), Spell Check, and Online Help are examples of buttons you can add to the Toolbar, saving you the trouble of selecting these options from the menus. You can use the Toolbar in message views as well as in the main GroupWise screen. (In Chapter 11, we explain how to customize your Toolbar.)

Toolbar

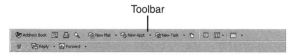

FIGURE 1.8
The Toolbar provides quick access to the most commonly used GroupWise functions.

CHAPTER 1 Introduction to GroupWise 6.5

Keystroke Shortcuts

Many of the options found in the pull-down menus can also be accessed by keystroke sequences, allowing you to efficiently perform GroupWise tasks without reaching for the mouse. For example, you can refresh the current folder's message listing by choosing the Refresh option from the View pull-down menu, or you can simply press F5 to get the same result. Not all functions have keystroke shortcuts. If a pull-down menu command has a keystroke shortcut, it is listed next to the function in the pull-down menu. A comprehensive list is available in Online Help.

QuickMenus

QuickMenus, shown in Figure 1.9, is a GroupWise feature that adds functionality to the right mouse button. When you are accessing different areas of the interface, a right-click of the mouse displays a short menu of actions that is relevant to the item or area you are clicking on.

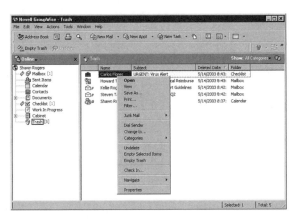

FIGURE 1.9
QuickMenus provides context-sensitive shortcut menus for common GroupWise functions.

QuickViewer

By enabling the GroupWise QuickViewer, you can read messages and view their attachments without double-clicking these items. A third, lower-pane viewing window displays the message that is highlighted, as shown in Figure 1.10. When you select a message in the Items Area, the main GroupWise screen's QuickViewer pane displays the message contents automatically.

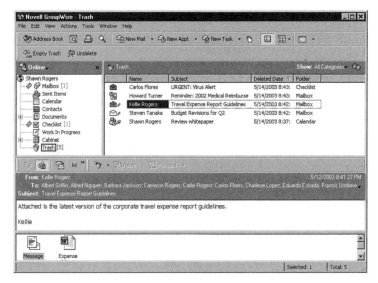

FIGURE 1.10
The QuickViewer provides an instant view of message contents.

Summary

In this chapter you learned about the GroupWise interface, which gives you access to many different messaging and calendaring functions, and you also learned some tricks that will help you navigate that interface. The next chapter explains the important new functions that appear in GroupWise 6.5.

CHAPTER 2

What's New in GroupWise 6.5

The GroupWise User program has several new features and enhancements. This chapter describes each one of them and shows how they can make your collaboration activities more productive.

The intent here is to provide a concise, brief overview of these features, not to delve into the details of each. We'll briefly describe each feature and provide a graphic of most of them. This should help users who are familiar with GroupWise quickly get up to speed on the new addition to the end-user interface.

This chapter is divided into three groupings of new features: look and feel, functionality, and management. Look-and-feel features are those that add to or change how the user accesses or utilizes functions within GroupWise. Functionality features are those that provide totally new capabilities for the user. Finally, management features enhance the user's ability to organize and keep track of the messages and information stored in GroupWise.

Look and Feel

The features in this section provide new ways for users to access information and functions with the GroupWise 6.5 program. These new features are numerous, so we have organized them in a fashion that will help you find what you need quickly. We also encourage you to try out these features on your own; for more detailed, step-by-step instruction, we include a reference to the chapter where each feature is covered in detail.

Read Views

When a message is received in GroupWise, a "view" is used to display the information within the program. Instead of using one view for both composing messages and reading incoming messages, it is now possible to define the view used to read messages. For example, you can send emails in the standard GroupWise format and open each email in the HTML (Web page) format. This allows for the use of fonts, colors, and embedded graphic images (JPG image files) or even Web content (an embedded Web page within the email itself), as shown in Figure 2.1.

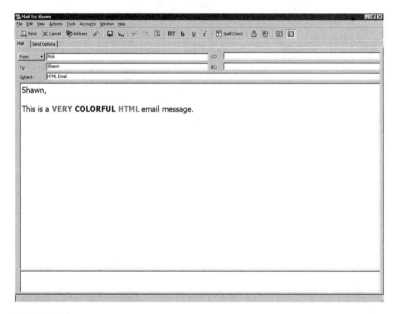

FIGURE 2.1
This HTML email message includes font colors and formatting.

New Headers

Headers are labels over a particular folder or information set being viewed. For example, if you are looking at the contents of the Mailbox folder, the header is the area that displays "Mailbox." The Show option is used to list a subset of the messages in that folder (the default set is All Categories, as shown in Figure 2.2).

Show option

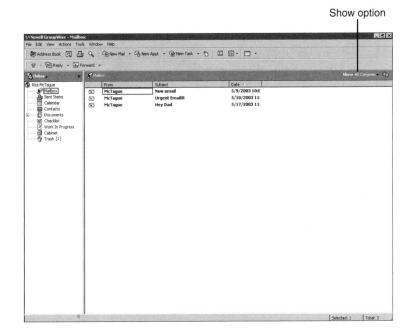

FIGURE 2.2
The Mailbox header area's Show option lets you select a subset of messages to view.

GroupWise 6.5 allows you to change the colors, fonts, and information in the header, providing tremendous customization. We will cover the steps to customize your headers in Chapter 11, "Customizing GroupWise."

TIP You can right-click in the header area to customize it.

Mode Selection

GroupWise 6.5 introduces a new way of choosing the mode to use for accessing the information stored in your mailbox—a new drop-down list.

NOTE GroupWise 6 had the mode selector in the Toolbar.

The three possible modes are online, caching, and remote. Without getting too technical, these modes are defined as follows:

▶ **Online**—GroupWise accesses the information directly from a post office, over a network.

▶ **Cache**—GroupWise synchronizes, over a network, the information between a local copy and the mailbox stored on your email server.

▶ **Remote**—GroupWise accesses the mailbox stored on your local hard drive (for example, on a laptop) and periodically synchronizes changes, over a network or the Internet, with your mail server.

NOTE Chapter 8, "Advanced Features," describes changing modes in more detail.

Changing modes is accomplished by simply choosing a mode from the drop-down list in the header, as shown in Figure 2.3.

The Mode drop-down list

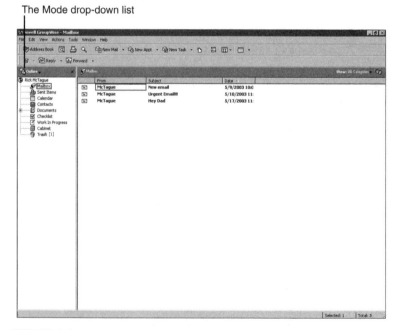

FIGURE 2.3
The drop-down list in the header area lets you select the mode.

Filter Enhancements

Filters are used to limit the display of information (messages, for example, in the Mailbox folder) based on some criteria, such as the message priority. This list has grown significantly in GroupWise 6.5 to about 54 different fields that can be used as filters.

NOTE Chapter 5, "Message Management," discusses using filters in more detail.

GroupWise 6.5 has added a symbol (see Figure 2.4) that enables you to quickly initiate the use of a filter. Simply click the symbol to select a filter for your messages.

Filter symbol

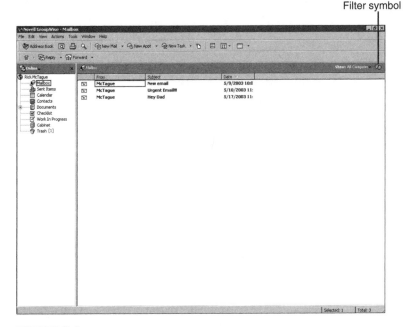

FIGURE 2.4
The filter symbol enables you to select a filter quickly.

Calendar Enhancements

Several new Calendar folder enhancements make it easier to select the day, week, month, or year to view (see Figure 2.5). At the far right of the header area above the Calendar information you'll find the following navigation buttons for changing to different views, while not changing to a different date:

- ▶ Day view (the "1" button)
- ▶ Week view (the "7" button)
- ▶ Month view (the "31" button)
- ▶ Year view (the "365" button)
- ▶ Multiuser view (the button with two figures)

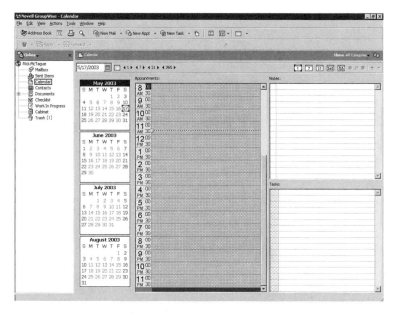

FIGURE 2.5
The Calendar folder includes new navigation buttons.

The left side of the header area allows for navigation to a different date, while keeping the same view. For example, the "7" arrows allow you to move backward and forward a week at a time.

Also, a date selector is available by clicking the symbol next to the date being displayed, and the button showing a "sunrise" takes you back to the current date. The Calendar folder, and its use, is covered in much greater detail in Chapter 6, "Personal Calendaring and Task Management."

Toolbar Enhancements

The Toolbar is a customizable area that provides single-click access to menu items—in other words, every GroupWise function can be made into a button that can be placed on the Toolbar. One key enhancement to the Toolbar is that it's now "dynamic"—the Toolbar changes to provide functions that pertain to the folder being viewed.

For example, while you're viewing the Contacts folder, the default Toolbar contains buttons that allow you to manage contacts (New Contact, New Resource, and so on), as shown in Figure 2.6.

NOTE Contacts are discussed in Chapter 4, "The Address Book and the Address Selector."

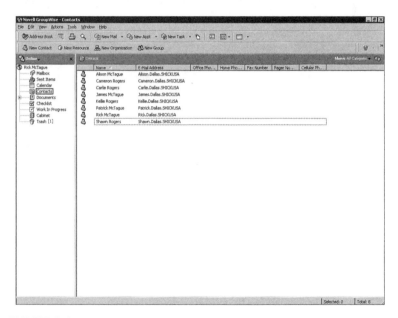

FIGURE 2.6
The Contacts folder has a different Toolbar than the Mailbox folder.

Another enhancement is new symbolic images (icons) for the functions in the Toolbar.

Functionality

This group of new features in GroupWise 6.5 adds capabilities not available in earlier versions of the program. These features provide more collaboration and information-management capabilities; Novell listened to what users wanted and responded with these very powerful new capabilities.

Categories

Categories (discussed more fully in Chapter 5) provide the ability to color-code messages, allowing you to group messages with common importance, action, or meaning. For example, a default category is *Urgent*, signified by the message in a folder being displayed in red instead of black (see Figure 2.7).

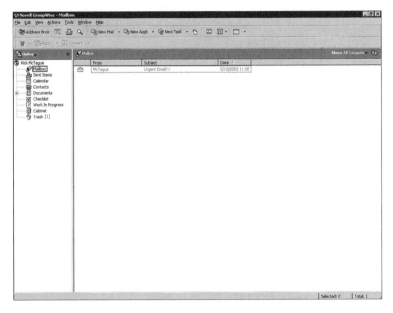

FIGURE 2.7
An Urgent category is used to mark a message needing immediate attention. Categories display in different colors in GroupWise.

You can create as many categories as you want. To change a message's category, or to add more categories, right-click any message, select

Categories from the pop-up list, and then click the category or choose the "More..." option.

My Subject

My Subject is an interesting new feature that allows you to change the subject of any message you've received to one that might make more sense or assist you in message management (such as changing the subject to one that will activate a rule).

NOTE My Subject is discussed in Chapter 8.

To change the subject of an email message, double-click the message and select the Personalize tab. Then enter a new subject and click the Close button.

The From Drop-down List

Because GroupWise allows access to multiple mailboxes (your corporate mailbox and a personal Internet mailbox, for example), the From feature was added, which allows you to easily select which mailbox you want the recipient to see as the message being sent from (Chapter 3 provides more detail on how to do this).

Address Selector

The Address Selector was added to allow quick access to addresses while composing a new message. When you click the Address button of a new message, the Address Selector is launched (see Figure 2.8).

This is the same information in your address books, but it's accessed much quicker than launching the full Address Book.

Address Book Enhancements

Many enhancements have been made to the GroupWise 6.5 Address Book, which is covered in detail in Chapter 4. The Address Book now sports a folder list, much like the main window of GroupWise itself, providing quick access to different address books. The headers and toolbars provide quick access to often-used functions, such as the Name Completion feature and adding new Address Book contacts, groups, or resources.

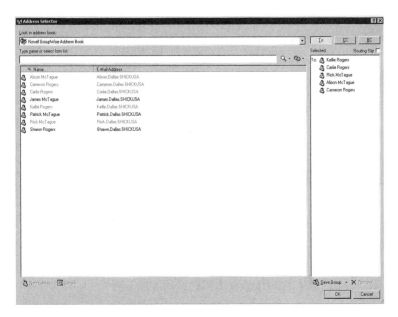

FIGURE 2.8
The Address Selector is used to quickly find message recipients.

Adding a new contact opens a much more detailed and information-packed contact-management dialog box, as shown in Figure 2.9.

It is now possible to track much more information about a particular contact, such as personal information, comments, and advanced security information (certificates), than was previously available.

NOTE You can use categories for your contacts by selecting the Categories button at the bottom of the New Contact dialog box.

Security Enhancements

Additional security is available in GroupWise 6.5 in the form of encryption and digital signatures. (These topics are discussed in more detail in Chapter 8.) The use of certificates and public/private keys is required for this feature, which essentially allows you to send encrypted messages over the Internet. The digital signature feature allows a recipient to ensure the message came from the purported sender. GroupWise 6.5 provides access to certificates from within the Address Book.

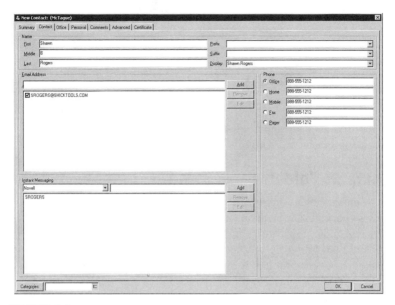

FIGURE 2.9
The GroupWise 6.5 New Contact dialog box has several fields for contact management.

Junk Mail Handling

With the massive increase in "spam" email (unwanted or unsolicited messages sent to thousands of recipients over the Internet), a significant need for dealing with these messages exists. Beyond the capabilities on the "server" side of the system, where the messages come in, GroupWise 6.5 provides a Junk Mail folder and a set of customizable rules that determines what is placed in that folder and what happens to the messages once placed there (see Chapter 8). From the Tools menu, click Junk Mail Handling to configure this feature.

iCal Internet Appointments

iCal is an Internet standard for appointments, and GroupWise 6.5 provides the ability to send appointments to Internet recipients in this format. If the receiving system is also "iCal aware," the appointment should be added to its calendar system as an actual appointment. Systems that are not iCal capable will simply display the appointment as an email with the appointment information (date, time, and so on). We will discuss this feature in more detail in Chapter 7, "Group Calendaring and Task Management."

Management

This section includes features and enhancements that provide new capabilities in organizing and accessing information. More effective information management with GroupWise is the goal of these features.

Contacts Folder

The Contacts folder provides a quick way to see the contacts in the address books from the main GroupWise screen. When you click the Contacts folder, the headers and toolbars change to allow you to quickly add and manage your contacts (without doing so from the Address Book). The Contacts folder is discussed further in Chapter 4.

Checklist Folder

GroupWise tasks—viewed in the Task List folder in previous versions—are items that need to be completed. In GroupWise 6.5, you can now easily place a message in this folder (via click and drag), creating a Checklist item (covered in more detail in Chapter 5). When combined with the Category feature, it is possible to create organized and grouped tasks from any message type (email, calendar entry, and so on).

Once an item is placed in the Checklist folder, you can verify that it has been completed by clicking the check box next to the entry.

Tabbed Item Views

When you open or an email message or calendar event, a set of handy tabs appears along the top of the message, as shown in Figure 2.10.

We'll discuss the send options in detail in Chapter 8, but as you can see from this figure, they can be easily accessed in a new email message on the Send Options tab. From here you can select a priority, classification, and so on.

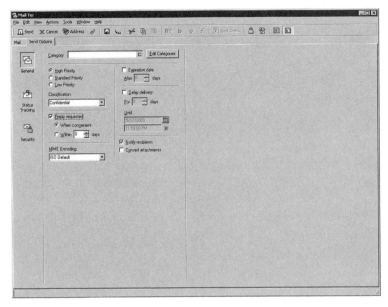

FIGURE 2.10
The Send Options tab provides quick access to message-configuration options.

Summary

In this chapter we looked at the new look and feel, functionality, and organizational features and enhancements of GroupWise 6.5. They were covered briefly to expose you to what is new. Chapter 3, "Messaging Fundamentals," will walk through the fundamentals of using GroupWise as a powerful email messaging client program.

CHAPTER 3

Messaging Fundamentals

Whether you have used email for years, are just beginning, or are curious to learn the easiest and most efficient ways to communicate electronically, this chapter will apply to you. Our goal is to provide a logical and productive set of tools for accessing, sending, reading, forwarding, replying to, and deleting messages.

This chapter teaches you the fundamentals of GroupWise 6.5 messaging. GroupWise 6.5 is more than just an email program; it is an Internet-enabled personal time manager, a group scheduler, a document-management system (that is, it can be used for managing word processing documents and other application data), a collaboration program (meaning it provides sharing of information between working groups), and an email program all rolled into one.

As you saw in Chapter 1, "Introduction to GroupWise 6.5," several types of GroupWise messages exist. Typically, these include mail messages, phone messages, appointments, tasks, and reminder notes; however, other types of messages are available in enhanced GroupWise systems. You can send all of these message types to other users. You can also use GroupWise messages to keep track of your own schedule. Keep in mind that proper use and management of all message types are essential to using GroupWise effectively.

GroupWise 6.5 uses icons to represent different message types and to reflect changes in the status of messages. By glancing at any icon in your mailbox, you can identify which type of message it represents. You can also tell whether the message has file attachments, what its priority level is, and whether you have already opened the message.

Figure 3.1 shows how different message icons appear in the GroupWise Mailbox folder when the corresponding messages are either opened or unopened. You should familiarize yourself with the different message icons so you can easily manage the different message types. Note the subject of each message in Figure 3.1.

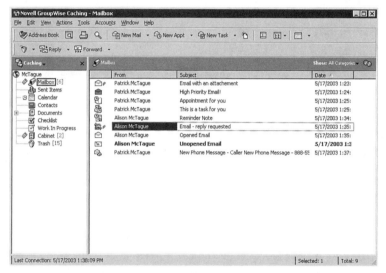

FIGURE 3.1
Different message types as they appear in the Mailbox folder.

Other visual clues give different kinds of information about messages. A paper clip next to a message indicates that the message includes an attachment (such as one or more files or a forwarded message that you can read once you open the email message). Two arrows indicate that a reply is requested. A red message icon indicates a high-priority message, and a gray message icon indicates a low-priority message. (We explain how to set message priorities in Chapter 8, "Advanced Features.") If the folder contains a reference to a document, spreadsheet, or other data stored in a GroupWise library, the icon reflects the application it is associated with. For example, a reference to a file with a `.doc` extension has a Microsoft Word icon, if your computer associates DOC files with that word processing application. (GroupWise document management is explained in Chapter 9, "Document Management.")

About GroupWise Accounts

One of the strongest features of GroupWise is the ability to centralize your different email accounts into one concise program. You can use GroupWise not only to access your company messages (also known as your *GroupWise mailbox*) but also to access personal or other email accounts, such as an AOL email account, using GroupWise 6.5. We will explain how to set up access to other email accounts in Chapter 8.

GroupWise Mailbox

Your company-established email account is known as the *GroupWise mailbox*. Each user in GroupWise has his or her own GroupWise mailbox. These mailboxes are usually created and managed by your company's IT department and stored on servers on your company's network. The GroupWise 6.5 client program is how you access this information. When you run GroupWise, you are typically accessing your GroupWise mailbox. Your company may have established email policies regarding the use of GroupWise.

Message Types

When you're talking about GroupWise, the word *message* has many different meanings. Different message types have different purposes. There are six basic message types in GroupWise 6.5: mail messages, appointments, tasks, notes, phone messages, and discussions. (Additional message types are available if you have an enhanced system, such as voice mail messages and fax messages. Check with your system administrator if you are not sure whether your system has enhanced capabilities.)

Discussing Mail Messages

A *mail message* (also called an *email message*) is like a memo. It has one or more recipients, a subject line, and a date. In addition, mail messages contain fields where you can specify recipients of carbon copies and blind carbon copies. We focus on mail messages in this chapter. The other message types are covered in detail throughout the rest of this book.

To create a mail message, click the New Mail icon on the Toolbar. Alternatively, you can select File, New, Mail from the menu bar.

NOTE Mail messages can be received from inside your GroupWise system (internal email messages) or from outside of your system (email from the Internet or another mail system). Once mail is delivered to your mailbox, GroupWise treats all messages the same.

Making Appointments

You can create two types of appointments: posted appointments and meetings. Posted appointments are entries you make in your Calendar to keep track of your personal engagements and to block out times in your Calendar when you are busy with important tasks or tentative appointments. Meetings are group appointments that you can use to schedule meetings with other GroupWise users.

When another user sends you a request for a meeting and you accept it, the meeting automatically moves to your Calendar. If you decline a meeting request, the message status information in the sender's Sent Items folder tells the sender that you have declined the meeting. Chapter 8 discusses how to set sending options for additional alerts when meetings are accepted or declined.

TIP Instead of using standard email messages to schedule meetings, create GroupWise meetings. Standard email messages do not automatically create entries in the recipients' Calendars. When you use standard email messages for scheduling, recipients must take the time to mark their Calendars with personal appointments.

GroupWise meetings include information such as the date, place, start time, and duration of the meeting. If you send a request for a meeting to a user outside of your GroupWise system (such as an Internet recipient), this information is converted into text placed inside of a regular email message, as shown in Figure 3.2.

GroupWise 6.5 uses the time zone of the sender in this converted message. This is important to remember if your company has several locations in multiple time zones. Previous versions of GroupWise would use the time zone of the mail gateway computer instead of the sender, resulting in some confusion as to the start time of the meeting.

To create a posted appointment, click the down-arrow button next to the Appointment icon on the Toolbar and then click Posted Appointment.

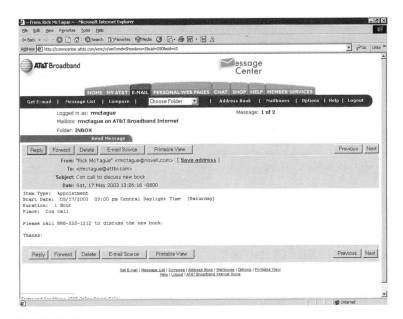

FIGURE 3.2
GroupWise meetings are converted to email messages when received by an Internet recipient.

NOTE Creating a posted appointment does not prevent others from scheduling you for meetings at that time; however, this action creates a scheduling conflict if they do a "busy" search on your Calendar.

To create a posted appointment, from the File menu click New and then Appointment. Alternatively, click the New Appointment button on the Toolbar.

Using Tasks

You can use a task message to delegate or assign tasks to other GroupWise users. You can also create posted tasks for your personal Task List.

NOTE Instead of using email messages to delegate assignments, send a task. Tasks automatically appear in the recipients' Task Lists, and you can conveniently specify a priority and a due date for each task.

When someone receives and accepts a task, the task appears in the recipient's section of his or her Calendar view. The task is carried forward each day until that person marks it as "completed." If the recipient does not mark a task completed by the specified due date, the task turns red in the Calendar view.

NOTE Tasks and the Checklist folder are somewhat related—you can use both for keeping track of items that you need to deal with. Tasks are not displayed in the Checklist folder unless they are placed there, via click and drag. The Checklist folder is discussed in Chapter 5, "Message Management."

To create a task, from the File menu click New, Task. Alternatively, you can just click the New Task button on the Toolbar.

About Reminder Notes

You can use reminder notes to create notes for yourself or to send reminders to other GroupWise users. When someone receives and accepts a reminder note, the reminder note automatically moves to the Notes field in the recipient's Calendar view. Unlike a task, however, a reminder note is not carried over from day to day. You enter reminder notes into the Calendar only on the date specified.

NOTE If you want to create a reminder note that appears regularly—for example, to remind yourself when payday comes around—you can use the Auto-Date feature. When creating a new note, select Auto-Date from the Actions menu and then click the dates for the recurring note. Auto-Date is further explained in Chapter 6, "Personal Calendaring and Task Management."

To create a personal reminder note, open your Calendar view and double-click inside the Notes field. To send someone else a reminder note, click File, New, Reminder Note.

Send reminder notes to members of your workgroup notifying them of days and times when you are away from your desk, in meetings, or on vacation. This action reminds the people in your workgroup where you are on the specified days.

Learning About Phone Messages

Use phone messages to inform other GroupWise users about phone calls you have taken for them. A phone message is similar to an email message. The Phone Message window includes fields for caller information (such as name, company, and phone number) and a description of the call (Urgent, Please Call, Returned Your Call, and so forth). GroupWise phone messages are basically electronic versions of preprinted phone message forms.

To create a phone message or "while you were out" message, click File, New, Phone Message.

Because phone messages are so similar to regular email messages, with the exception of the fields in the view, we do not discuss them further.

NOTE A *discussion* is a special type of message that you use with Shared Folders. They show topics and the response threads to those topics. We explain discussions in Chapter 8.

Message Formats: HTML Versus Text

GroupWise allows you to send and receive both "plain-text" messages (messages composed in text, with limited formatting and content) and HTML messages. HTML messages look very similar to regular GroupWise messages, they just use a different view with an additional toolbar for formatting, as shown in Figure 3.3. HTML messages enable you to embed HTML documents (Web pages) and information in the message body and then send them to the recipients.

To create an HTML message, click File, New, Mail. From the New Mail Message screen, click View, HTML. You can retrieve an HTML file into a new email message by using File, Retrieve and selecting the HTML file.

Working with URLs

You can easily embed Web page addresses (URLs) in both the subject line and message body area of an email. These URL links become "live." In other words, with a click of the mouse on these links, your computer's Web browser will open up, pointed to that Web page.

NOTE This option is available in both the plain-text and HTML views.

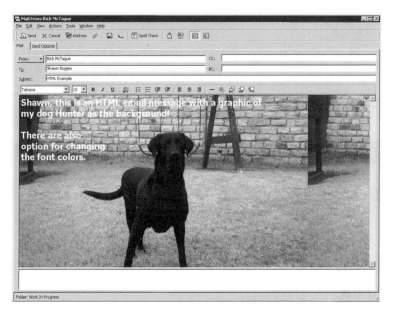

FIGURE 3.3
GroupWise allows you to send Web page content inside of HTML messages.

Alternate Email Views

Views are display formats for GroupWise messages and interface components. For example, a mail message has two views associated with it: Mail and Simple Mail. You can choose a view that excludes the features you don't need or one that has a larger-than-normal message area.

NOTE Using alternate views does not prevent you from using all the GroupWise features. In alternate views, you may not see certain shortcut (right-click or Toolbar) methods for activating features, but you can always use the pull-down menus to access those features.

The Simple Mail view provides a concise message area without the CC and BC buttons and the shortcut buttons to send, cancel, address, and attach files, as shown in Figure 3.4. Choose the "Mail (Simple)" option on the New Mail drop-down list on the Toolbar. Use this view when you need to send a short message to someone.

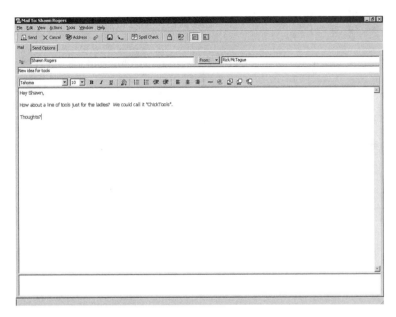

FIGURE 3.4
The Simple Mail view offers the basics of an email message.

Sending Messages

The GroupWise dialog box for sending messages is very easy to use. The
Message dialog box is essentially a form you complete for each message
you send. Although the different message types may have different fields
to fill in, several fields are common to all message types. In this section
we focus on sending email messages, but the concepts are basically the
same for all GroupWise message types.

To send a message, you must enter someone's email address. This might
be an Internet email message, such as `jimbo@shicktools.com`, or another GroupWise user in your company, such as `srogers`. GroupWise also
has a neat feature known as *Name Completion*. If you begin typing someone's name in the To, CC, or BC line, GroupWise looks at the Address
Book and tries to finish the name for you automatically. For example, if
you were sending a message to Susan Alexander, you might type "Susan
Al" and GroupWise would automatically finish the name for you.

TIP Any name or address field in GroupWise will use Name Completion.

Perhaps the most common method is to use the Address Book or Address Selector to enter one or more user addresses. (Chapter 4, "The Address Book and the Address Selector," covers the Address Book in depth.)

Figure 3.5 shows the new email message screen.

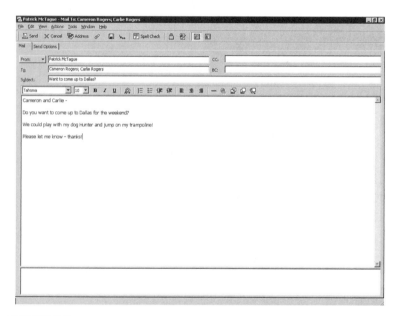

FIGURE 3.5
Sending a new email is as easy as filling out a form.

To send an email message, follow these steps:

1. Click File, New, Mail. Alternatively, you can click the New Mail button on the Toolbar.

2. Select the recipients using the Address Book or by typing their names in the To, CC, and BC fields. (Notice how the names complete automatically, as mentioned previously!) Press Enter after each name is complete. (Multiple names are separated with a semicolon.)

3. Add a subject line in the Subject field.

4. Type your message in the message area.

5. Click the Send button to send the message.

NOTE The Send Options tab is for adding additional features to the message, such as high priority. These are discussed in Chapter 8.

The recipients listed in the To field are the primary recipients of the message. Recipients listed in the CC field are the carbon copy recipients, and the BC field holds blind copy recipients. Recipients in each of these fields can see the recipients listed in the To and CC fields. However, none of the recipients can see recipients listed in the BC field; even blind copy recipients themselves cannot see the others listed in this field when they receive the message.

If you want to send a message to multiple people, but you don't want any of them to know who else received the message, make them all blind copy recipients. For example, you could use this technique to inform job applicants that a position has been filled if you don't want the applicants to know who else applied for the job. Because a name in the To field is required, you can insert your own name.

Attaching a File to a Message

You can share documents, spreadsheets, database files, and other types of files by sending them to other users as *file attachments* to a GroupWise message. You can attach files to any GroupWise message, even if the message type does not include a file attachment field in the dialog box.

To attach a file to an email message, follow these steps:

1. In the Email dialog box, click the Attach button.

2. Select the file to attach.

3. Click OK. The file attachment appears in the file attachment window, as shown in Figure 3.6.

TIP Instead of using the dialog box method described previously for attaching a file, you can attach files using Windows Explorer. Open Windows Explorer; open a new mail message, complete the address, subject, and message body areas, and arrange the New Mail Message window where you can also see Windows Explorer. Click to highlight the file (or files) in Windows Explorer and drag them to the attachments area of the new message. With a little practice, you should find this to be a powerful method of attaching files.

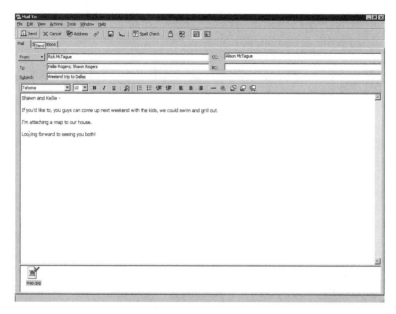

FIGURE 3.6
Attaching files or objects to messages allows you to share information with recipients.

You can also attach document references and object linking and embedding (OLE) objects, such as charts and spreadsheets, to GroupWise messages. In Chapter 9 we explain how document references work. To attach an OLE object to a GroupWise message, follow these steps:

1. From the new email message screen, click File, Attachments, Attach Object.

2. The Insert Object dialog box appears, as shown in Figure 3.7. Choose the Create New radio button to create a new object using the associated application; a list of the object types you can create is displayed. (Choose the Create from File radio button to select a preconfigured object, such as a chart.)

3. Select the object type and click OK to open the application.

4. Create the object you want to embed in the native application.

5. In the application, click File, Exit and Return to GroupWise.

6. Select Yes to update the object into your message view.

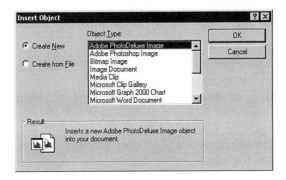

FIGURE 3.7
You can create objects or select existing objects to attach them to a new message.

The object you either selected or created is displayed as an icon in the attachments area of the new message. The attached file or object travels along with your message to the recipient.

The From Drop-down List

One thing you might notice in the new message screen is a drop-down list (selection list) on the From field. This allows you to change who you are sending the message as. For example, if your manager has given you proxy rights to send messages on his or her behalf (discussed in Chapter 8), you can select your manager's name in the From drop-down list. The message will appear to the recipients no differently than if your manager had actually sent the email.

If you have access to multiple email accounts, your other accounts will also be listed as possible "From" candidates.

Using Internet Addresses

Entering an Internet recipient's email address in the To, CC, or BC field is as simple as typing it in directly or selecting it from the Address Book. If you have an entry in the Address Book for an Internet recipient, you can also enter the "display name" (usually first name/last name) until Name Completion finishes the name. This method avoids forcing you to type out the sometimes cumbersome Internet email addresses.

Saving Draft Messages in the Work In Progress Folder

As you compose a message, you might find a need to save your work and resume your message later. You can save messages you are working on in the Work In Progress folder. This is especially handy for long, complex email messages.

To save a message in the Work In Progress folder, follow these steps:

1. With the message open, choose Save Draft from the File menu.

2. Select the Work In Progress folder by verifying that the folder is highlighted. Then click OK.

TIP An alternative way to save a message in the Work In Progress folder—when you decide you need to work on a message later—is to click the Cancel button or press the Escape key on your keyboard. You are prompted to save the message. Choose Yes, and save the message in the Work In Progress folder.

To resume working on a draft message, follow these steps:

1. Open the Work In Progress folder.

2. Double-click the message you want to finish.

3. Finish the message and choose Send.

A message can be saved as a draft message at any point during its composition. You can also attach files to a message; they are saved along with the message in the Work In Progress folder.

NOTE If you modify a file that is attached to a message in the Work In Progress folder, be sure you delete the file attachment icon and reattach the message. Otherwise, the file's original version is sent.

Reading Messages

The messages you receive are initially stored in your Mailbox folder. New messages are displayed in bold. Here's how to read a message:

1. Click the Mailbox folder to display a list of the messages you have received.

2. Double-click the desired message, or highlight the message and press Enter.

The message opens for you to read. Note that the message's sender (if it was sent from within your GroupWise system) is able to see the "opened" status of your message. Message status is discussed in Chapter 5.

TIP Use QuickViewer to quickly read several messages in succession. To activate QuickViewer, click View, QuickViewer. A third pane opens at the bottom of the GroupWise window and displays the contents of the messages as they are selected, as shown in Figure 3.8.

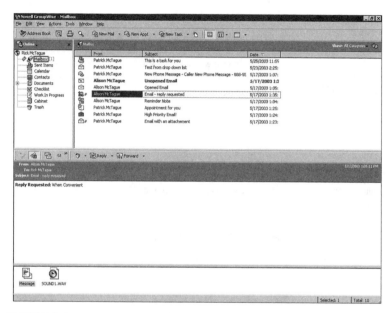

FIGURE 3.8
QuickViewer displays the contents of the messages in a third pane.

TIP The Personalize tab that is present when you are reading a received message allows you to change the Subject line of the message to one that you select. Enter a new subject in the My Subject field and click Close. My Subject is discussed further in Chapter 8.

Working with Attachments

When you receive a message with a file attachment, you have several options: You can view the attachment's contents, open the application

CHAPTER 3 Messaging Fundamentals

associated with the attachment, save the attached file to your hard drive, or print the attachment.

Viewing Attachments

You can easily view the contents of an attachment by simply clicking the attachment. The message window will then display the contents. To return to the original message, click the Message icon in the attachments area.

NOTE If the attachment is an email message itself (for example, a series of forwarded emails), GroupWise 6.5 allows you to select whether you want each forwarded message to open in a single window or in its own window. You will be prompted to select this option the first time you open a message that is attached. You can change this selection using the Options selection under the Tools menu.

To open the attachment in its own window, double-click the attachment icon.

NOTE The first time you view an attachment by double-clicking it, GroupWise prompts you to indicate what function you want double-clicking to launch, as shown in Figure 3.9.

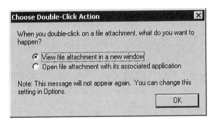

FIGURE 3.9
You select the default action the first time you double-click an attachment.

You can choose to have attachments open in their default application (choose Yes for the Environment option) or in the GroupWise viewer (choose No for the Environment option). If you change your mind later, you can adjust this setting using the Options feature under the Tools menu.

If you decide to use the GroupWise viewer, a new window opens, displaying the contents of the attachment.

NOTE The first time you view a file attachment in this way, GroupWise generates the viewers for all supported file formats. GroupWise only generates the viewers the first time you view an attachment after GroupWise is installed (or if you have installed updated viewer files), and it usually takes less than a minute to generate them.

From a viewer screen, you can launch the associated application or save the attachment.

Finally, you can choose to open an attachment in its default application. Double-clicking the attachment will open the application with the file open and ready to work with.

Saving File Attachments

When you receive a file attachment, you can easily save it to your file system. The following methods can be used to save attachments:

▶ Right-click the attachment icon, choose Save As, and specify the location where you wish to save the file.

▶ From the File menu, choose Save As, select the attachment, and specify the filename (in the Save File As field) and location (in the Current Directory field).

NOTE The default location for "Current Directory" is the directory where GroupWise is installed.

▶ Open Windows Explorer; arrange the open message window to where you can also see Windows Explorer. Click the file attachment and drag it to the target folder in Windows Explorer. With a little practice, you should find this to be a powerful method of saving files.

Printing File Attachments

You can print attachments either directly from GroupWise or from the associated application. You will need to experiment with both methods to find out which one works best for you. Here are two methods to print an attachment:

▶ Right-click the attachment icon, choose Print, click the attachment in the Items to Print list (shown in Figure 3.10), and click Print. To use the application to print the attachment, select the Print Attachment with Associated Application check box.

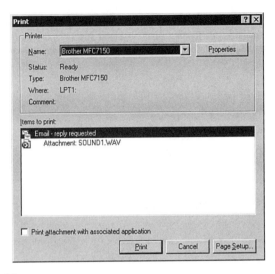

FIGURE 3.10
The Print dialog box allows you to print the message and/or any attachments.

▶ From the File menu, choose Print, highlight the attachment in the Items to Print list, and click Print. To use the application to print the attachment, select the Print Attachment with Associated Application check box.

TIP Use the Page Setup button to configure page orientation, margins, paper size, and paper source.

Replying to Messages

When you respond to another person's message, you can reply to the sender only or reply to all recipients of the message. You can also include the original message in your reply. When you include a copy of the original message, you can insert your comments at the top of the message or at various points throughout the message. Figure 3.11 shows the "message reply" options.

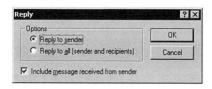

FIGURE 3.11
The Reply dialog box lets you select the recipients of your reply.

To reply to a message, follow these steps:

1. While the message is open, select a reply option from the drop-down list next to the Reply button on the Toolbar. You can also choose the Reply option under the Actions menu.

2. Choose either Reply to Sender or Reply to All, and specify whether you want the original message included.

3. By default, the Include Message Received from Sender option is selected. Deselect this option if you do not want to include a copy of the original message in your response.

TIP Use the Reply to All option judiciously. Make sure that everyone who received the original message really needs to see your reply.

The sender's name (and all recipients' names if you selected Reply to All) automatically appears in the To field. The original message's Subject field is retained, with the abbreviation "Re:" in front of it. If you left the Include Message Received from Sender option selected, the original message text appears in the reply message. When you type your reply, it appears above the original message unless you move the cursor to another location. Complete your reply and click the Send button on the Toolbar.

Reply messages do not automatically include the file attachments from the original message. You can, however, attach files to a reply message.

Forwarding Messages

If you want to pass along a message or its file attachment to someone else, you should forward the message. When you forward a message, you send a new message with the old message either embedded in the new message or as an attachment. The original message remains intact, along

CHAPTER 3   Messaging Fundamentals

with its file attachments, as shown in Figure 3.12. It is a good idea to
always include your own introductory message when you forward a
message.

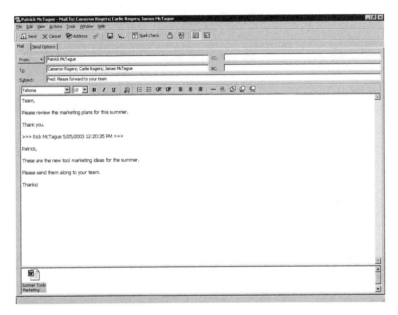

FIGURE 3.12
Forwarding a message sends the entire contents, including attachments, to
additional people.

You can easily forward messages that you receive to other recipients by
using one of the following options:

▶ From the Mailbox list of messages, right-click a message (or select
multiple messages via Ctrl+click or Shift+click) and choose
Forward as Attachment. This will create a new email message with
the selected messages attached.

▶ From an open message, select an option from the drop-down list
next to the Forward button on the Toolbar.

NOTE "Forward" will place the contents of the forwarded message into the body of the
new message. Attachments are always included when forwarding. "Forward as
Attachment" will leave the new message's body blank and will place the forwarded message as an attachment.

▶ From the Mailbox list of messages, select a message (or select multiple messages via Ctrl+click or Shift+click) and choose either Forward as Attachment or Forward from the Actions menu.

Regardless of the method you choose, a new message will be sent with the contents of the forwarded message. Fill in the recipient names in the To, CC, and BC fields, as appropriate, and type your subject line (the default subject line is the original message's subject with "Fwd:" in front of it). Then type an introductory message and click the Send button on the Toolbar.

When you forward a message, you actually create a new message that contains a copy of the original message *and* its file attachments. A copy of the original message remains in your mailbox. You can delete the original message if you don't need it, or you can store it in a folder.

When a recipient opens the forwarded message, he or she accesses the original message and its file attachments by double-clicking the mail message icon in the Attach field.

Deleting Messages

When you no longer need a message, you can delete it from your mailbox or any folder. After you delete it, the message goes to the Trash folder. The message remains there until you empty the Trash manually or until the Trash is emptied automatically, according to what you set up in GroupWise Options (see Chapter 8).

To delete a message, select the message and press the Delete key. Alternatively, you can click the message and drag it to the Trash folder.

You can delete messages from any location (for example, from the Mailbox folder, the Sent Items folder, or from any Calendar view).

Restoring Messages

When you delete a message, it goes to the Trash folder and stays there until you empty the Trash—or until your Trash is automatically emptied according to the default options that are set for your GroupWise account. While the message is stored in the Trash, you can undelete or restore the message to its original location.

To restore a message to the location it was deleted from, follow these steps:

1. Open the Trash folder.

2. Highlight the message.

3. Choose Undelete from the Edit menu.

Alternatively, you can right-click the message and choose Undelete. The message is restored to its previous location.

Purging Messages

To permanently delete a message, you can open the Trash folder and delete the message. You can also empty all messages from your Trash by right-clicking your Trash folder and selecting Empty Trash.

In previous versions of GroupWise, once messages have been emptied or deleted from Trash, they are no longer recoverable. With GroupWise 6.5, if the administrator runs a backup that contains messages and then restores that backup to a defined restore area, the user can use the client to connect to the backup area and look for messages by choosing File, Open Backup, as shown in Figure 3.13. You will need to contact your system administrator for specific information about how to restore messages from a backup.

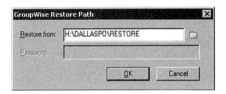

FIGURE 3.13
You can restore your mailbox from backup.

Summary

In this chapter we discussed the fundamental methods of sending, reading, replying to, and performing other actions on messages. We covered different message types as well as saving, printing, deleting, restoring, and purging messages. These features allow you to really manage messages as you create and receive them. In Chapter 4, we will dive deep into the GroupWise 6.5 Address Book.

The Address Book and the Address Selector

The GroupWise Address Book is your GroupWise "yellow pages"; it's your master directory for looking up information about other users. Using the Address Book, you can find other users' phone numbers, fax numbers, departments, and much more. It is also the primary tool for managing your contacts.

The Address Book is actually an independent software application that is tightly integrated with the GroupWise client. It can be launched independently of GroupWise to function as a corporate directory tool.

If you are familiar with previous versions of GroupWise, you will find that the GroupWise 6.5 version of the Address Book has a new look and feel. The Address Book has an entire new interface, patterned after the main GroupWise screen or Windows File Explorer. Individual address books now display in the left pane of the Address Book view, and you can use the + and – buttons to expand and collapse each Address Book.

NOTE When we refer to the *Address Book* (capitalized) we mean the Address Book program that is part of GroupWise. When we refer to *address book* (lowercase), we are referring to one of the individual directories—such as the system address book or the Frequent Contacts address book—that contains lists of users.

Also new to GroupWise 6.5 is a feature called the *Address Selector*, which is a simplified display of the Address Book that's shown when you are working with GroupWise messages (for example, when you are creating an email message).

Both the Address Book and the Address Selector pull their data from the same source in the GroupWise system.

In this chapter we'll first discuss the functionality of the Address Book and the most common tasks you will perform therein. Then we'll discuss the Address Selector and explain the techniques you can use when addressing messages.

You can use the Address Book and the Address Selector components of GroupWise 6.5 to do the following:

▶ Send messages to groups of users (for example, to all members of a specific department)

▶ Create personal groups that list the users to whom you often send messages

▶ Look up information about other GroupWise users, such as phone numbers

▶ Create personal address books that contain addresses of users within and outside the GroupWise system, such as people you commonly correspond with on the Internet

To access the Address Book from within GroupWise, click the Address Book icon on the GroupWise Toolbar or click the Tools menu and select Address Book. To access the Address Book outside of GroupWise, click Start, Programs, Novell GroupWise, GroupWise Address Book. The Address Book displays as shown in Figure 4.1.

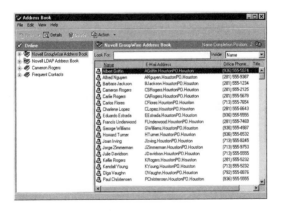

FIGURE 4.1
The GroupWise Address Book displays information about users.

Introducing Address Book Features

The redesigned GroupWise Address Book is streamlined for easy navigation and efficiency in locating users, contacts, and resources. Here are the Address Book's main components:

- ▶ Address book list
- ▶ Menus
- ▶ Search fields
- ▶ Information field headings
- ▶ Address book membership list

Figure 4.2 shows the GroupWise Address Book with its main components labeled.

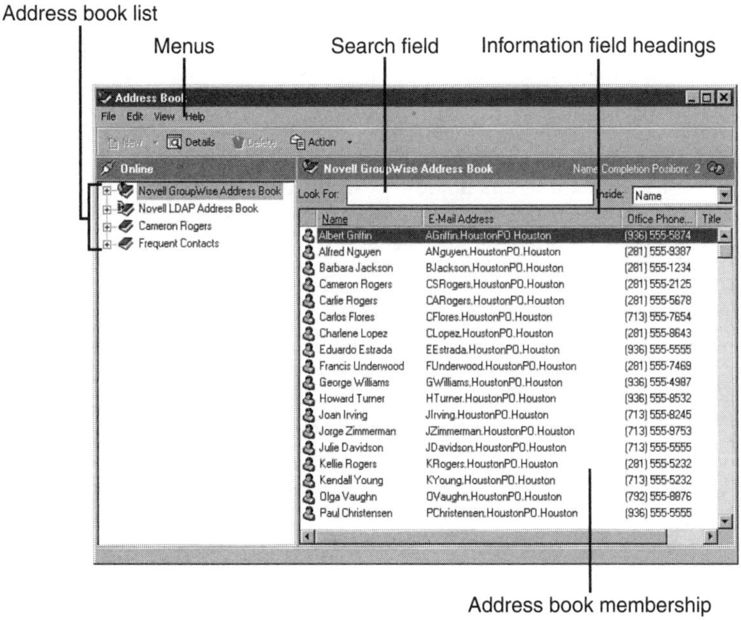

FIGURE 4.2

The GroupWise Address Book components provide access to the main Address Book features.

Notice in Figure 4.2 that, by default, the Address Book has four address books:

- ▶ Novell GroupWise Address Book
- ▶ Frequent Contacts aaddress book
- ▶ Novell LDAP Address Book
- ▶ An address book with your GroupWise username

The Novell GroupWise Address Book (the system address book) is the master address book for your GroupWise system. All users, groups, and resources in the system are visible in this address book (unless some of these have been purposely hidden by the administrator).

The Frequent Contacts address book lists all the users to whom you have previously sent messages or from whom you have previously received messages. These users are listed in alphabetical order. The Frequent Contacts address book lets you send messages quickly to the people with whom you correspond most often.

The Novell LDAP Address Book is a special address book that lets you use LDAP services available on the Internet to search for individuals and their email addresses. Once you locate an individual using LDAP services, you can add him or her to your other GroupWise address books.

The address book with your name on it is a personal address book that you use to add names, email addresses, and other personal information about people with whom you correspond. The users, groups, resources, and organizations listed in your personal address book do not have to be individuals within the GroupWise system (or even email users, for that matter). You can use your personal address book to store all your contact information. Later in this chapter, we'll explain how to create additional personal address books.

To switch between the various address books, simply click the address book in the left pane. If you don't want one of the default address books to display, you can highlight the address book and click File, Close Book.

You can change the way the address book membership information is displayed by moving or modifying the headings. To move a heading from one location to another, simply click and drag the heading to a new location. To remove a heading, click and drag the heading from the headings bar. To replace a heading that has been deleted, right-click the headings bar and select the heading you want to add. You can resize headings by clicking and dragging the line that separates two headings.

You can use two methods to obtain more information about an individual listed in an address book. First, you can simply move your mouse pointer over the name and let it rest for about a second, and a pop-up window will display details about the user. Second, you can right-click a name and select Details. A separate window will open that gives extensive details about the individual, as shown in Figure 4.3. (If some information is not displayed, the GroupWise system administrator has not populated all the available fields in the master directory.)

FIGURE 4.3
The Address Book user details dialog box provides information about individuals in the address book.

Addressing Messages with the Address Book

You can use the Address Book to initiate GroupWise messages to others. (Usually you will initiate messages from the GroupWise client and use the Address Selector to address the message, which is explained later in this chapter.)

To initiate a GroupWise message from the Address Book, highlight the user or users in the membership list and click the Action button on the Toolbar to launch a preaddressed email message. Alternatively, you can click the down arrow next to the Action button to select a different message type.

Managing Groups

A GroupWise *group* (also known as a *distribution list* in previous versions of GroupWise) is a list of users to whom you can send messages. Two address book types exist: public groups and personal groups.

A public group is a list of users defined by the system administrator for convenient message addressing. All GroupWise users have access to the system's public groups, unless the system administrator has limited access. For example, your system administrator may create a group called Sales that includes all members of the sales organization. Public groups are located in the system address book.

A personal group is a list of users you create to automate message addressing. For example, you can create personal groups that include the members of each project you work on. (Personal groups only display in personal address books. They do not display in the system address book.)

Groups are listed in the Address Book along with individual users. They are distinguished from users by a group icon, as shown in Figure 4.4.

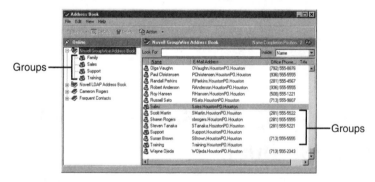

FIGURE 4.4
Groups in the Address Book are represented by a special group icon.

Notice in Figure 4.4 that you can expand the address book in the left pane to reveal all the groups available. If you highlight one of the groups in the left pane, the group members display in the membership area.

Addressing Messages to Groups

To address a message to a group from within the Address Book, follow these steps:

1. Open the Address Book.

2. Highlight the group in the membership list (right pane).

3. Click the Action button on the Toolbar or click the down arrow next to the Action button and select a message type.

To search for groups, simply begin typing the group's name in the Look For field. When GroupWise finds the group you want, it will complete the name and you can stop typing. This feature is known as *Name Completion* and is available in several areas of GroupWise, including the To line when composing a message.

If you want to send a message to most, but not all, group members, expand the address book listing in the left pane and highlight the group. Then use Ctrl+click to select individuals in the group (in the right pane) and click the Action button.

Creating Personal Groups

You can create personal groups that appear in your personal address book or in your Frequent Contacts address book. To create a personal group, follow these steps:

1. Right-click your personal address book or your Frequent Contacts address book in the left pane and then select New Group. Enter a name for the group.

2. Click the address book that contains the users you want to add to this group (most likely the Novell GroupWise address book).

3. Locate the first user you want in the group and then click and drag that user into your new group. Repeat with all additional users.

You can include users from different address books in one group.

Creating Personal Address Books

Personal address books give you additional flexibility in organizing lists of individuals who you correspond with most often. Personal address books can contain users who are in the GroupWise system or contacts who are external to the GroupWise system, such as Internet users. (Remember, the Novell GroupWise address book and the Novell LDAP address book are system address books and only the administrator can add to or modify these lists.) You can create an unlimited number of personal address books within the Address Book to organize your contacts.

By default, GroupWise creates one personal address book for you. Your personal address book has your name on the address book line.

To create a new personal address book, do the following:

1. With the Address Book open, click File, New Book.

2. Name the new address book and choose OK. The address book name appears in the left pane.

3. Click the New button.

4. Choose Contact, Group, Resource, or Organization.

5. Fill in the fields for the entry.

6. Click OK.

TIP To quickly add users from the Novell GroupWise address book to a personal address book, use Ctrl+click to select multiple users, then right-click, choose Copy To, and select your personal address book as the destination.

Keep in mind the following points about personal address books:

▶ You can create, edit, and save any number of personal address books.

▶ You can add and delete names and address information for any person, resource, or organization in your personal address books, but you cannot modify information in the system address books.

▶ The same name can be included in multiple address books. If you copy an entry from one address book to another and then later modify the entry, the entry is updated in all address books that contain it.

- ▶ Internet addresses can be included in personal address books.

- ▶ You do not have to display all address books in the Address Book main window. To choose which books you want open, use the Open Book and Close Book options in the File menu to specify which address books appear.

- ▶ You can define custom fields for your personal address books. See the topic "Create My Own Fields and Columns" in the Address Book Online Help system for instructions.

TIP To send a message to everyone in a personal address book, click the address book tab to make the address book active. Then choose Edit, Select All (or press Ctrl+A), and click the Action button.

To edit an entry in a personal address book, simply double-click the entry. You can edit the fields of the entry and click OK to save the changes.

Here's how to delete a personal address book:

1. Click File.

2. Click Delete Book.

3. Highlight the book or books you want to delete.

4. Click OK.

5. Click Yes to confirm the deletion.

Remember, the deletion of a personal address book is permanent, and it cannot be restored once deleted.

Searching the Address Book

You can search for Address Book information by using the Search List box, by using a predefined address filter, or by defining your own filter.

Using the Search List

To search for an address using the Search List, follow these steps:

1. Click the tab of the address book you want to search.

2. In the Search List box, begin typing what you are searching for. GroupWise places information that matches your search criteria in the resulting search box.

Figure 4.5 shows the Search List box.

Address book search

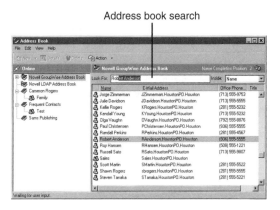

FIGURE 4.5
Address Book search fields allow you to quickly find individuals in the address book.

Predefining Address Filters

In GroupWise, a *filter* is a set of conditions that remove selected items from being displayed in a list. For example, you can use a message filter to stop unopened messages from appearing in your mailbox, or you can use an address book filter to display only resources or groups. You learn more about using filters in Chapter 5, "Message Management."

By default, address books display all entries that have been incorporated into them. Consequently, in large address books, individuals and groups can be difficult to locate. By using a predefined filter, you can display only the information you are looking for.

The Address Book has four predefined filters: Filter for Groups, Filter for Contacts, Filter for Resources, and Filter for Organizations. In addition, you can define your own customized address filters.

To use a predefined filter while using the Address Book, follow these steps:

1. Click View.

2. Click one of the predefined filters displayed in the menu.

After you enable filtering, a dot appears next to the selected filter in the View menu, and a filter icon appears in the upper-right portion of the Address Book display. Only the individuals, groups, organizations, or resources specified in the filter appear in the address list.

Figure 4.6 shows the GroupWise Address Book filtered to show only groups. Notice that the filter icon appears next to the Name Completion Position text in the upper-right portion of the Address Book.

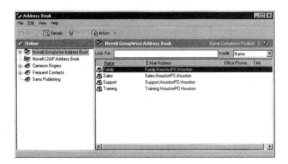

FIGURE 4.6
Address books can be filtered to show only groups.

To return to the regular (nonfiltered) Address Book view, click View and then click the Filter Off option.

Learning About User-Defined Filters

You can design customized filters to help you with common address book searches. For example, if you often send a message to all managers in a company, you might define a filter that searches for all managers. By using this filter to send a message to managers, you ensure that the message is sent to people with that title.

Using customized filters is often more efficient than creating personal groups because groups quickly become outdated. A filter ensures that only current users in the address book receive your message.

To create a filter, follow these steps:

1. Click View.

2. Click Define Custom Filter. The Building a Filter dialog box appears. The first column lists the filter criteria available in the address book.

3. Click a criterion.

4. Click the Operator drop-down box to select an operator.

5. Type a parameter in the Parameter text box. By default, the Parameter drop-down box displays End.

6. If you want to choose additional parameters, click the Parameter drop-down box and choose an operator.

7. Repeat Steps 3 through 6 to establish additional filter criteria.

8. When you have defined the filter, choose End in the final parameter's drop-down box and then click OK.

An *operator* is a symbol that represents a mathematical operation. A *parameter* is a variable used with a command to indicate a specific value or option. For example, to create a filter that lists only users with the last name Williams, click the Last Name column, click the equal sign (=) button, and then type **Williams**. In this example, = is the operator and Williams is the parameter.

Here is another example. Suppose you want to create a filter that addresses a message to everyone in your company's sales department. Follow these steps:

1. Click View.

2. Select Define Custom Filter.

3. Click the Column drop-down list and select Department.

4. Click the Operator box and choose =.

5. Enter the department's name (for example, Sales) in the Parameter box.

6. Choose OK to apply the filter.

Figure 4.7 shows the Building a Filter dialog box for the previous example.

FIGURE 4.7
Custom filters allow you to select only specific items for display in the
address books.

Sharing Personal Address Books

You can easily share an address book you create with other GroupWise
users, who can then use the address book themselves.

Suppose you maintain an address book for a specific department. You
can share the department address book with other users by following
these steps:

1. Create the custom address book and populate it with the user
   information.

2. Click File, Sharing. The Sharing dialog box displays.

3. Click the Shared With option, as shown in Figure 4.8.

FIGURE 4.8
Personal address books can be easily shared with other GroupWise users.

4. Enter the names or groups with which this address book should be
   shared in the Name field.

5. Specify the access rights the user should have. In most cases, the
   recipients of your shared address book only need read access.

NOTE If you grant full access rights to the shared address book, the recipient can read, add, edit, and delete entries in the address book.

6. Click OK. A dialog box appears enabling you to customize the message that the recipient of the shared address book receives.

7. Click OK to share the address book. The recipients receive a message indicating that you have shared an address book with them. They have the opportunity to accept or decline the shared address book.

Once you share an address book, the people you share it with can see all the items within it—no other steps are necessary. If you add, change, or delete entries, the users you shared the address book with also see those changes.

As an alternative to sharing an address book, you can use the Address Book's export and import features to share specific items within any address books with other users. This is handy for sharing this information outside of your organization, because you can only share address books within the GroupWise system.

Here's how to export an address book:

1. Open the address book you wish to export.

2. Click File, Export.

3. Choose Entire Address Book or Selected Items.

4. Name the address book file. (Address book export files have an .nab file extension.)

5. Choose Save.

You can now send this file to other users as an attachment to a message. They can then import the file.

To import a personal address book file, follow these steps:

1. Highlight the personal address book to which the group is imported, or create a new personal address book to contain the imported users.

2. Click File, Import.

3. Locate the NAB file and choose Open.

You cannot import users into the system address book.

Integrating The GroupWise Address Book with Other Systems

GroupWise supports integration with other vendors' address books. For example, if your system supports another email program, you might be able to use that email program's address book along with the GroupWise Address Book.

Here's how to integrate another vendor's address book in GroupWise:

1. Open Control Panel.

2. Double-click the Mail icon.

3. Select Add.

4. Follow the prompts to add the vendor's address service.

You should contact your system administrator to determine whether you can use another vendor's address book with your GroupWise program.

TIP The dialog box you see after Step 2 of the previous list is also the dialog box you use to determine the order in which address books are searched by the GroupWise Name Completion feature.

Using the Address Selector

The Address Selector's functionality is very similar to the Address Book's functionality. Many of the same tasks can be accomplished in the Address Selector. The Address Selector is simply a modified view of the Address Book, optimized to perform the tasks most commonly used when addressing messages.

The Address Selector only appears when you are generating a message in GroupWise, when you select the Address function from the Toolbar or from the Actions menu, and in other areas within the GroupWise client program when you need to select users. The Address Selector is shown in Figure 4.9.

The Novell GroupWise address book is the default address book that is displayed. You can select any of your other address books by clicking the drop-down menu.

CHAPTER 4 The Address Book and the Address Selector

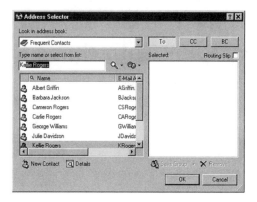

FIGURE 4.9
The Address Selector displays when you're addressing GroupWise messages.

TIP When addressing a message, if you are sure about how to spell a user's name and don't want to use the Address Selector, you can simply begin typing the user's name in the To, CC, or BC field, and GroupWise uses the Name Completion feature to make a best guess about which user you want. When the correct name appears, simply tab to the next field.

To address a message with the Address Selector, use the arrow keys or the scrollbar to locate an addressee and then double-click the user's name to insert that name in the Address Book's To field. Insert any additional names and then choose OK to return to your message. The recipients are inserted in the message's To field.

Instead of trying to scroll through a long address book, you can quickly find an addressee by simply beginning to type the person's name. The address list quickly highlights the name that most closely matches what you type.

The right column (where the users are listed when you select them from the Address Book) defaults to the To field. GroupWise assumes that most users you send the message to are the primary recipients and should be added to the message's To field. Consequently, when you select users from the address list, they are listed in the To field by default. To add BC or CC recipients, click the corresponding button before adding users.

If you have a user in the To field who needs to be moved to either the CC or BC field, you can right-click the user name and choose the appropriate field from the QuickMenu. Alternatively, you can hold the Ctrl button down, select multiple names that need to be moved to either CC or BC, and then click the CC or BC button.

TIP If you want to route the message to the recipients in a sequential order, click the Routing Slip check box above the To field in the address book. You can then click and drag the recipient names to your desired routing order. This lets you create a simple workflow formessages or documents that should go to recipients in a specific order. (Note: If the Routing Slip option is selected, you cannot create new personal groups, as explained in the next subsection.)

Creating a New Personal Group with the Address Selector

After you have selected the individuals to whom you will send the message, it is common to want to save that distribution list for future use. The Address Selector allows you to save the group you have built to one of your personal address books.

To save a group, follow these steps:

1. Use the Address Selector to populate the To, CC, and BC fields.
2. Click the drop-down list to select a personal address book.
3. Click the Save Group button.
4. Name the Group.
5. Click OK.

NOTE By default, the group will be listed in your Frequent Contacts address book. You will probably want to select a personal address book for the new group.

Summary

This chapter explained how to use the GroupWise Address Book and the GroupWise Address Selector to automate mail message addressing and to organize information about people with whom you frequently correspond. In the next chapter, you will learn how to effectively manage messages using GroupWise.

CHAPTER 5

Message Management

Electronic communication, once thought of as basic email, is growing to become the mission-critical application for many organizations. The use of collaboration systems such as GroupWise is definitely on the rise, as is the amount of information that users send and receive on a daily basis.

In addition, as messaging technology advances, more and more message types are being created. In a standard GroupWise 6.5 system, the Mailbox displays mail messages, phone messages, discussions, contacts, appointments, tasks, notes, and documents. In addition to the messages in your corporate GroupWise system, you might be using GroupWise as a mail client for additional Internet mail accounts, such as AOL. With GroupWise add-on products, the Mailbox can also display other kinds of messages, such as fax messages, voice mail messages, and workflow action items.

With all these different message types available, you need some way to manage your messages, to prevent information overload, and to eliminate clutter from your GroupWise Mailbox. In addition, locating information quickly is a key need. This chapter explains how to use different GroupWise features to organize, manage, and locate your messages.

We've organized this chapter into three main areas: working with folders in the Cabinet (creating, sharing, and using folders); working with messages you receive (finding, filtering, saving, archiving, printing, deleting, and organizing using the Checklist and Categories); and working with the messages you send (checking the properties, resending, and retracting).

Organizing Messages with the Cabinet

You use the Cabinet to organize and store your message folders. You can organize folders in the Cabinet the same way you organize directories in DOS or Windows 3.1, or folders in Windows 95/98/2000/XP and on the Mac OS.

The folders in your Cabinet fall into five categories: personal folders, shared folders, find results folders, IMAP folders, and NNTP folders.

You create personal folders for your own, private use. Use them to organize your messages and documents into separate groups. For example, you can create folders for information pertaining to certain projects, for specific message types, or for messages from certain individuals.

You can also create shared folders, which contain messages that can be viewed by other users. A shared folder's creator determines the access rights to the folder. For example, when you create a shared folder, you can decide who is permitted to read the messages in the folder, who can add messages to that folder, and so forth.

Find results folders are used to display a fresh listing of items that are the results of a Find session. For example, a High Priority Items folder can do a fresh search of your entire mailbox for messages that have a priority of High. Each time you click this folder, the search is performed again, so the listing is updated. The Find tool is covered later in this chapter.

NOTE The Sent Items and Checklist folders are "system" folders and cannot be deleted.

IMAP folders are used when accessing an IMAP 4 mail account on the Internet with the GroupWise client. Enabling this feature is discussed in Chapter 8, "Advanced Features."

NNTP folders are used to store messages received from Internet newsgroups. Setting up NNTP access with the GroupWise client is also discussed in Chapter 8.

Creating Folders

GroupWise folders work the same way as the subdirectory structure of your computer's hard drive. When you open GroupWise 6.5, your folders appear on the left side of the screen. Your name should automatically appear on the top-level folder (the user folder). In addition to your user folder, eight default GroupWise folders exist: Mailbox, Sent Items, Calendar, Documents, Checklist, Work In Progress, Cabinet, and Trash.

You can only add new folders in the Cabinet, in your user folder, in the Documents folder, and in the Work In Progress folder. You cannot create subfolders under any Find results folder (such as Sent Items or Checklist), under the Calendar, under Trash, or under the Mailbox folder. We recommend that you store most of your GroupWise messages in Cabinet folders. You can organize the folders and subfolders in your Cabinet any way you like.

NOTE In GroupWise, folder names can include punctuation and spaces.

Figure 5.1 shows some typical folders. A button with a plus sign to the left of a folder indicates that the folder contains hidden subfolders. A button with a minus sign to the left of a folder means that the folder has been expanded to show all its subfolders. Click a + or - button to show or hide the substructure beneath a particular folder.

To create a folder, follow these steps:

1. If you want to create a folder that extends directly from the Cabinet folder, highlight the Cabinet folder. (If you want to create a sub-folder under another folder, select the folder under which you want to create the subfolder.) You can also highlight the Work In Progress folder to create subfolders underneath it.

2. Choose File, New, Folder.

TIP You can right-click the folder and choose New Folder from the QuickMenu.

---

3. Select the type of folder you want to create from the list—Personal, Shared, or Find Results—and then click Next. IMAP and NNTP folders are discussed in Chapter 8.

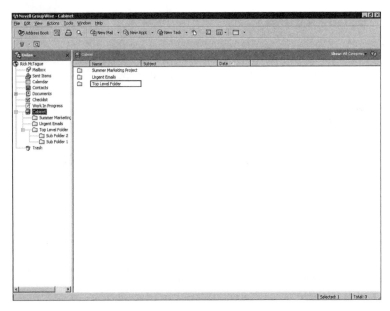

FIGURE 5.1
You can create folders to help organize messages.

4. Enter a folder name that describes the folder. You can use the Position area and the buttons at the right of the dialog box (Down, Left, and so on) to adjust the placement of the folder, as shown in Figure 5.2.

   If you want to move a folder later, simply click it from the main screen and drag it to where you want it.

5. Click Next to continue creating the folder. You see the settings dialog screen, as shown in Figure 5.2.

6. You can change the description, the item source and type, the default view and sort, and the column information for the folder. Once you have personalized these choices, you can save them by clicking the Save As button and naming the folder configuration, as shown in Figure 5.3.

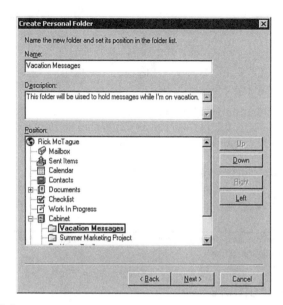

FIGURE 5.2
You can enter a lengthy description of new folders as they are created.

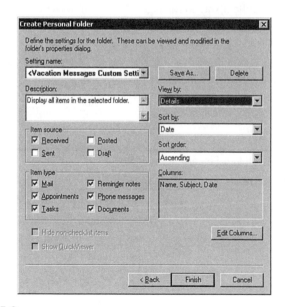

FIGURE 5.3
Folders can be highly customized using the options in this dialog box.

TIP You can choose from a list of predefined folder settings in the Setting Name drop-down list.

---

7. If you are creating a personal folder, click Finish to create the folder. (Shared folders are discussed later in this chapter.)

8. If you are creating a find results folder, you see the Find dialog box, as discussed later in this chapter. Enter the Find criteria and click Finish to create the find results folder.

As you create folders, you can change the settings later by editing the properties of the folder. Highlight the folder, click the right mouse button, and choose Properties.

NOTE We explain more about how to customize the Cabinet and its folders in Chapter 11, "Customizing GroupWise."

Sharing Folders

When you create a folder in GroupWise 6.5, you can easily share it (and its contents) with other people in your system. This feature, called *shared folders*, is an excellent way to manage information that pertains to many people. For example, your company might have a shared folder called *Company Notices* to store messages intended for the entire company.

As mentioned before, the creator of the shared folder controls access to it. In the Company Notices example, a few key people might receive Add privileges (to add messages to the folder), and everyone else would be given Read privileges. Table 5.1 explains the different kinds of access privileges.

TABLE 5.1 Shared Folder Access Privileges

ACCESS PRIVILEGE	DESCRIPTION
Read	View and read messages in a folder
Add	Add messages to a folder
Edit	Modify items in a folder
Delete	Delete items from a folder

To share a folder, follow these steps:

1. Highlight the folder you would like to share. (If you select a folder that has subordinate folders, only the selected folder is shared, not the folders underneath it.)

2. Choose Sharing from the File menu. The Sharing tab opens, and the Not Shared option is highlighted. Alternatively, right-click and choose Sharing from the QuickMenu.

TIP When you create a new folder, you can choose Shared Folder as the type of folder you wish to create.

---

3. Select Shared With and enter the names of the users you would like to share the folder with, or click the browse button next to the Users field to open the Address Selector. If you open the Address Selector, double-click the users or groups you wish to share this folder with. (Choosing a group means sharing with all members of the group. You can set the permissions for each person, as described next.) Click OK.

4. From the Sharing properties page, highlight a user from the list (or select multiple users with either Shift+click or Ctrl+click), and choose the access privileges you want that person to have. All users added to the Sharing list receive Read access by default. (Add allows users to place items in the folder, Edit enables users to change the items in the folder, and Delete enables users to erase items from the folder.)

5. Click OK.

6. The Shared Folder Notification screen appears. All new participants are displayed, and a mini message screen appears. Fill in the Subject line, enter a short message, and click OK.

Your Shared Folder Notification message automatically is sent to the participants, informing them about their access to the shared folder. The people you shared the folder with receive a Shared Folder Notification message in their Mailbox. Each recipient needs to install the shared folder. To do this, follow these steps:

1. Double-click the Shared Folder Notification message in your Mailbox folder. You see the Install Shared Folder Wizard start (see Figure 5.4).

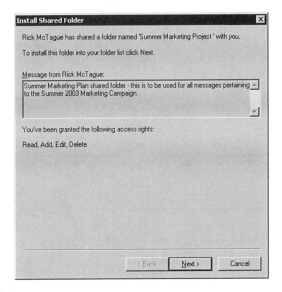

FIGURE 5.4
Recipients of a shared folder will receive this notification to install the folder.

2. Read the summary information and note the rights that you have been granted to this shared folder. Click Next.

3. The Install Shared Folder Wizard lets you name the folder whatever you'd like and place it in your individual structure of folders wherever you'd like. Use the Up, Down, Right, and Left buttons to move the folder. Click Finish to install the shared folder.

TIP When you install a shared folder from someone else, it is represented by a little man facing to the left (your folders). If you create a shared folder, the man is blue and is facing toward the right (items).

You can use shared folders to move mail from one user to another. This would be useful for directly exchanging a large group of messages, rather than forwarding them individually. Following are the steps involved (for this example we define the *source user* as the one whose mail is to be moved, and the *target user* as the user who is to become the new "owner" of that mail):

1. The source user shares a folder (or folders) containing the mail to be moved. The target user is added to the access list and granted all rights.

2. The target user accepts the shared folder or folders.

3. The target user drags all items from these shared folders to other folders in his own Mailbox.

4. After waiting for the move-to-folder operation to complete (usually just a minute or two), the target user deletes the shared folders.

5. The source user may now delete the shared folders. Note that when the source user looks in these folders (before deleting them), all the items in them are gone.

Deleting Folders

To delete a folder, follow these steps:

1. Select the folder to be deleted.

2. Choose Edit, Delete. (Alternatively, you can right-click the folder and choose Delete from the QuickMenu.) A summary of the messages in the folder appears, as shown in Figure 5.5.

FIGURE 5.5
When you delete a folder, you will see a summary of its contents.

3. Choose whether to delete only the messages or both the folder and its messages.

4. Click OK.

Renaming Folders

To rename a folder, follow these steps:

1. Select the folder to be renamed, right-click it, and then choose Rename from the QuickMenu.

2. Edit the folder name and press Enter.

TIP You can use the Folders option under the Edit menu to determine which folders open in the main GroupWise screen when you start GroupWise. You can also use this dialog box to move folders up or down in the listing of folders, to create new folders, and to rename folders as shown in Figure 5.6.

FIGURE 5.6
The Folders dialog box is an alternate method of managing your folders.

NOTE The folder list can be sorted manually using the Folder Manager, or you can click the folder you wish to move and drag it to its destination.

Managing Messages Using Folders

Two different ways exist in which you can place a message in a folder: by moving it there or by linking it to the folder. When you move a message to a folder, the message is actually stored in that folder.

To move a message into a folder, do the following:

1. Expand folders (if necessary) by clicking the button with a plus sign (+) to the left of the folder. The target folder needs to appear in the folder tree.

2. Click the message in the Items Area and drag it into the target fold-er. The message is now stored in that folder. If the message was previously stored in a different folder, it no longer appears there.

When you link a message to a folder, a copy of the message is placed in the destination folder. Once this is done, you can see the message in the original folder and in the folder to which the message has been linked. Any modifications to the original message (for example, changes in the appearance of the message icon) are reflected in the folder to which the message has been linked.

Follow these steps to link a message to a folder:

1. If necessary, expand the folders by clicking the plus sign to the left of them.

2. Hold down the Ctrl key on your keyboard, click the message, and drag it from the original folder into the target folder. The message is now stored in both the original folder and the folder to which the message has been linked.

You can also use the dialog box shown in Figure 5.7 to move and link your messages to folders. To access this dialog box, highlight a message and choose the Move/Link Selections to Folders option under the Edit menu.

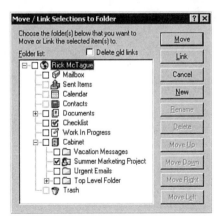

FIGURE 5.7
Use this dialog box to move or link messages to folders.

Using Message Threading in a Folder

When you use message threading, you can view the whole history of messages and replies behind a particular message. Message threading has many uses. You can follow workflow as it develops and see the development of collaboration. You can also go back and review certain steps in a long process. Figure 5.8 shows message threading.

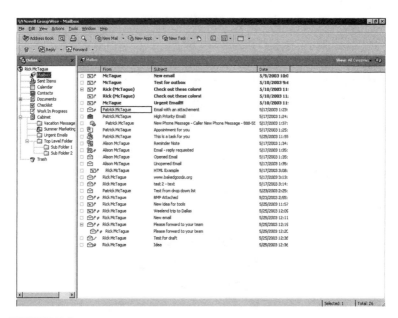

FIGURE 5.8
Message Thread views allow you to see the replies to messages in a historical fashion.

Follow these steps to enable message threading in a folder:

1. Open a folder by clicking it.
2. Click View, Display Settings, Discussion Threads.

Now you see all the messages and their replies in a particular folder.

TIP Message threading is particularly useful when viewing *discussions* in a shared folder. Shared folders were discussed earlier in this chapter, and discussions are covered in Chapter 8.

Finding Messages

The GroupWise Find utility is the main tool used to look for and locate messages and documents throughout your Mailbox and any document-management library you have rights to. Documents are different from other message types in that they are stored in libraries and are accessed using the program, document, spreadsheet, or graphics file the document is associated with. Using Find to look for documents is covered in Chapter 9, "Document Management."

Find is a simple-yet-powerful utility that returns a results window; this is similar to any lookup system, such as locating a book by a particular author on a Web site. The results from the search can then be read, deleted, moved to a folder, saved, printed, or archived, just like any other message.

To start a Find session, simply click the Find option in the Tools menu, or click the magnifying glass icon on the Toolbar. The Find by Example tab is opened first.

You can create very simple requests to find items. For example, the Find by Example request shown in Figure 5.9 looks for mail messages that have the word *meet* in the Subject line or anywhere in the message's contents (that is, a *full text* search).

NOTE Previous GroupWise versions opened to the full Find tab. GroupWise 6.5 opens to the Find by Example tab.

TIP The "From" and "To, CC" search fields in the Find by Example dialog box use the Name Completion feature and the Address Book (discussed in Chapter 4, "The Address Book and the Address Selector") to complete the names for the search.

All folders and libraries are searched. Once the Find criteria has been specified in this screen, click OK to execute the search. The GroupWise Find Results screen displays (see Figure 5.10), listing the messages and items that are found.

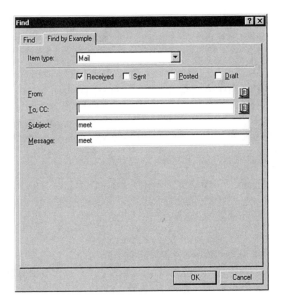

FIGURE 5.9
The Find by Example tab is used to search for messages based on criteria
you enter.

Once the results have been displayed, you can act on the messages just
like you would normally, or you can perform any other action, such as
moving the messages to a folder.

TIP As you see later in this chapter, you can save the results of a Find operation as a
find results folder, which performs the search every time you access the folder's contents.

A more in-depth search can be created using the Advance Find tab and
filters, which are discussed in depth later in this chapter. Figure 5.11 is
an example of using the Find tab for a Find session that looks for all
phone messages sent to Cameron Rogers. Notice that the Mailbox (and
any folder underneath) can be selected in the Look In area of this screen,
as well as libraries.

FIGURE 5.10
Find results are displayed and can be acted upon in this screen.

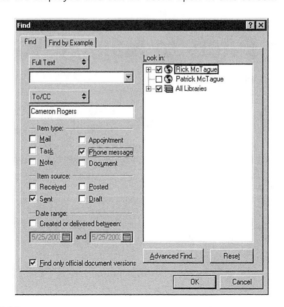

FIGURE 5.11
Find is highly customizable to meet any search requirements.

To add more criteria to the Find session, select other items, such as message type, who the message was from, the disposition of the message (sent, received, and so on), and a date range for the age of the message. To add advanced search criteria beyond what is available in this dialog box (such as message priority of high), click the Advanced Find button and you can craft a search that can boggle the mind.

The Advanced Find dialog box (see Figure 5.12) is exactly like the Filter dialog box, which we cover later in this chapter.

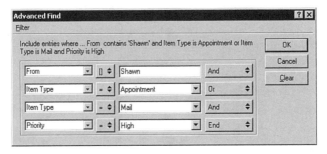

FIGURE 5.12
Advanced Find allows you to make a complex search for messages.

Using Filters to Manage Your Messages

You can use filters to screen out certain messages when viewing them in any GroupWise folder. For example, you can apply a filter to your Mailbox that displays only your Mail and Phone messages, or a filter that displays only your unopened messages. You can save the filters you create and use them again later.

Here are some situations in which a filter can be very useful:

▶ You have a lot of messages in your Mailbox, and you want to see only unopened messages.

▶ You want to see only messages that were received during a specific period of time (for example, from January 1, 2003 to February 1, 2003).

▶ You want to see only messages you received from a specific person.

▶ You want to see only high-priority messages.

▶ You want to see only messages that contain a certain keyword in the Subject field.

A filter does not remove messages from your Mailbox; it only determines which messages are displayed. When you close a filtered display, the filter is automatically removed. The next time you open the same folder, all the messages appear again. The exception to this is if you used a filter from the predefined list of filters. In such a case, the filter stays active.

NOTE Remember, a filter limits the messages displayed in a folder based on your criteria. Find uses a filter to generate a list (Find Results) of messages that meet the criteria.

Filter Terminology

You should understand five key terms exist before you begin working with filters:

▶ Filter topic

▶ Filter qualifier

▶ Filter variable/constant

▶ Filter group

▶ Filter terminator

Filter Topic

The *filter topic* is the part (or parts) of a message you want considered when GroupWise determines which messages to display. The following list shows the various filter topics from which you can choose:

▶ Account

▶ Annotation

▶ Assigned Date

▶ Attachment List

▶ Attachments

▶ Author

▶ Caller's Company

▶ Caller's Name

- ▶ Caller's Phone Number
- ▶ Category
- ▶ CC
- ▶ Copy Type
- ▶ Created
- ▶ Date Opened
- ▶ Delivered
- ▶ Document Created Date
- ▶ Document Creator
- ▶ Document Number
- ▶ Document Type
- ▶ Due/End Date
- ▶ Filename Extension
- ▶ From
- ▶ Item Source
- ▶ Item Status
- ▶ Item Type
- ▶ Library
- ▶ Message
- ▶ My Subject
- ▶ Number Accepted
- ▶ Number Completed
- ▶ Number Deleted
- ▶ Number Opened
- ▶ Number Replied
- ▶ Opened By
- ▶ Place
- ▶ Posted By
- ▶ Priority
- ▶ Send Options

- ▶ Size

- ▶ Started

- ▶ Subclass

- ▶ Subject

- ▶ Task Category

- ▶ Task Priority

- ▶ Thread State

- ▶ To

- ▶ Total Recipients

- ▶ Version Created Date

- ▶ Version Creator

- ▶ Version Description

- ▶ Version Number

- ▶ Version Status

- ▶ View Name

Filter Qualifier

The *filter qualifier* is the logic component of a filter; it indicates the selections to be made. Each filter topic has a different list of available qualifiers. For example, Less Than applies to the filter topic Size, whereas Begins With is applicable to the filter topic From, but not to Size.

The following list shows the different filter qualifiers:

- ▶ Contains

- ▶ Begins With

- ▶ Matches

- ▶ Includes

- ▶ Does Not Include

- ▶ Equal To

- ▶ Not Equal To

- ▶ Less Than

- ▶ Less Than or Equal To

▶ Greater Than

▶ Greater Than or Equal To

▶ Equal To Field

▶ Not Equal To Field

▶ Less Than Field

▶ Less Than or Equal To Field

▶ Greater Than Field

▶ Greater Than or Equal To Field

▶ On

▶ Before

▶ On or After

▶ After

▶ On or After Date

▶ On or Before

▶ On Date

▶ On or Before Date

▶ After Date

▶ Before Date

Filter Variable/Constant

A *filter variable* is the input on which GroupWise bases message filtering, such as a user's name. A filter constant sets the parameters of the filter topic. For example, High is a filter constant for the filter topic Priority; Phone Message is a filter constant for the filter topic Item Type.

Filter Group

A *filter group* is a single, complete decision line in one filter. The formula for filter groups is explained in the section "Building a Filter" later in this chapter.

Filter Terminator

The *filter terminator* determines what kind of action GroupWise takes once it has made the proper selections. Table 5.2 explains the different filter terminators available.

TABLE 5.2   Filter Terminators

TERMINATOR	ACTION
And	Adds an "And" condition to a single filter group
Or	Adds an "Or" condition to a single filter group
Insert Row	Adds an additional condition row in a single filter group
Delete Row	Deletes a condition row in a single filter group
Insert Group	Adds an additional filter group
End	Terminates the filter

Building a Filter

When you build a filter, you specify the criteria GroupWise uses to determine which messages to display. The formula for this decision appears in the Advanced Filter dialog box, as shown in Figure 5.13.

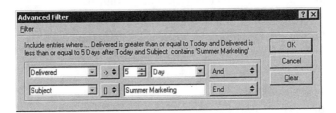

FIGURE 5.13
The Advanced Filter dialog box allows you to build filter scenarios.

The formula for building a filter is as follows:

Include entries where <Filter Topic> <Qualifier> <Variable/Constant>

Here's an example:

Include entries where Items Type = Phone Message

This filter displays only Phone messages in the folder.

A *simple filter* is a single-decision filter. A *complex filter* is one where multiple decisions can be evaluated. The Filter Terminator field in the far-right side of the Advanced Filter dialog box enables you to add more than one decision.

The filter in Figure 5.14 displays only high-priority messages received from Rick.

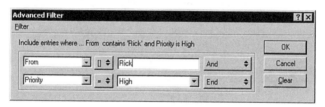

FIGURE 5.14
This is a more complex filter with multiple conditions.

To apply a filter to a folder, follow these steps:

1. Open the folder and click View, Filter, Edit/Create.

2. Select the display criteria and choose Save (if you want to use this filter again). You need to specify a filter name and click the Put On menu option to add this filter to the menu.

   If your filter does not display any items, you see the dialog box shown in Figure 5.15.

3. Click OK to apply the filter.

FIGURE 5.15
If no items match your filter criteria, you will see this notification.

If you want to use a previously created filter, follow these steps:

1. Click View, Filter.

2. Select the filter you would like to use and click OK. The folder now displays only the filtered messages.

To return to your normal, unfiltered view, right-click in the filtered folder and choose Clear Filter from the QuickMenu.

TIP You can use filters to locate messages. For example, if you know that John Smith sent you a message, but you can't find it among your many messages, create a filter that screens out all messages except those from John Smith. This only works if you know what folder the message is in. Otherwise, you are going to be better served with a Find operation.

Archiving Messages

The primary method for storing messages indefinitely is called *archiving*. An archived message is not stored in your master Mailbox (which is on a GroupWise server); rather it is stored on your local hard drive or in your user directory on the network. Archiving messages gives you access to your old messages without cluttering up your master Mailbox. You can archive messages that have been sent to you as well as messages you have sent to others. The process of archiving messages is fairly easy. In fact, you can set up the GroupWise 6.5 client so that archiving happens automatically when messages have been sitting in your master Mailbox for a certain period of time.

NOTE You can archive messages when using GroupWise Remote; you cannot using the GroupWise WebAccess.

TIP Because GroupWise can access multiple email accounts, you can use the archive feature to store your Internet mail account messages locally.

Before you can archive messages, you must specify a location where your archived messages are stored. This location is usually on your hard drive. If you have questions about your archive directory's location, ask your system administrator. Here are the steps to follow:

1. Click Tools, Options.

2. Double-click the Environment icon and choose the File Location tab, as shown in Figure 5.16.

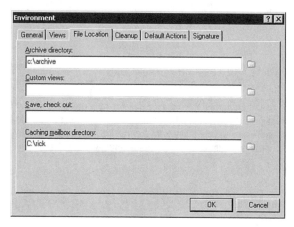

FIGURE 5.16
The archive path specifies the location for archive files.

3. Enter a directory path in the Archive Directory field or browse to a directory on your hard drive by clicking the file symbol next to the Archive Directory field.

4. Click OK and then Close.

To archive messages, follow these steps:

1. From a folder (for example, the Mailbox or the Sent Items folder), select a message or group of messages. (You can select a range of messages by pressing Shift and clicking the beginning and end of the range. You can select multiple, nonadjacent messages by pressing Ctrl and clicking the messages.)

2. Choose Actions.

3. Choose Move to Archive.

The selected messages move to your local archive storage file.

TIP Optionally, you can right-click the message or group of messages you want to archive and choose Move to Archive from the QuickMenu.

To have GroupWise automatically archive messages after a certain length of time, click Tools, Options, Environment, Cleanup. (See Chapter 11 for customizing these options.) You can adjust the period of time that mail messages, phone messages, appointments, tasks, and notes remain in your Mailbox before they are automatically archived. Automatic archiving then takes place as needed each time you exit GroupWise.

Viewing Archived Messages

To view an archived message, follow these steps:

1. Select File and then choose Open Archive. The messages stored in the Archive mailbox are listed. As Figure 5.17 illustrates, the text *(Archive)* appears on the title bar to indicate that you are looking at archived messages. If you view the File menu again, you see that a check mark appears next to the Open Archive option. The check mark indicates that the archive is currently open.

2. Double-click the message you want to read. If you are using the QuickViewer (see Chapter 1, "Introduction to GroupWise 6.5"), the contents of the archived message appear in the bottom message pane.

NOTE The folders you have created in your server-based master Mailbox for organizing your messages are replicated to the archive storage when a message in those folders is archived. This includes the replication of "nested" subfolders. We discuss creating folders later in this chapter.

To return to your Mailbox from an archive, click File and then deselect Open Archive. The active folder and its contents appear. If you look at the File menu again, you see that no check mark appears next to the Open Archive option. The check mark disappears when the regular Mailbox is active, and (Archive) disappears from the title bar.

Unarchiving Messages

To unarchive a message or group of messages, do the following:

1. With your Archive mailbox open, select the message or group of messages you want to move back to your active Mailbox.

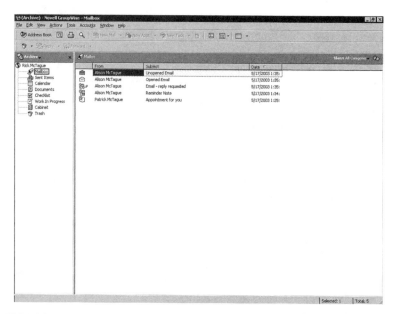

FIGURE 5.17
The GroupWise window's title bar displays *(Archive)* to denote archive access.

   2. Click Actions and then deselect Archive. (The Archive option is a
      toggle switch. When a message is archived, a check mark appears
      next to the Archive option in the File menu.)

The selected messages are removed from your hard drive on a
GroupWise server. You should now be able to see the messages in their
original folder.

Saving Messages

Saving messages is different from archiving. When you save a message,
you transfer the message information into a separate file.

TIP You can also save the message to a GroupWise library. Document management is
covered in Chapter 9.

This file can then be used in a word processing program or other application. When you archive a message, the message is not deleted from your Mailbox; GroupWise merely saves a copy of it in a separate file.

To save a message, follow these steps:

1. From the Mailbox folder, select the message and then choose Save As under the File menu.

2. As shown in Figure 5.18, highlight the message, specify the destination directory and filename for the message, and click Save to save the message as a file. The message is saved as a WordPerfect-compatible document. A default filename is created from the Subject field (you can create your own filename).

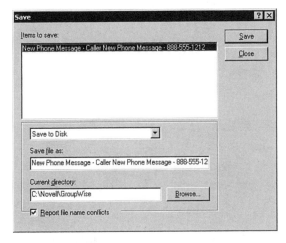

FIGURE 5.18
You can save GroupWise messages to your file system using this dialog box.

NOTE Previous GroupWise versions saved messages with the `.mlm` extension; GroupWise 6.5 does not specify an extension.

When you save a message as an individual file, it does not maintain the properties on the item (such as priority or security), and the formatting is similar to what you get when you print the message.

The default directory for this dialog box is the "Start In" directory for the GroupWise Windows shortcut. Changing that directory to the desktop can be a big productivity boost for folks who use the Save feature often. Change this by right-clicking the Windows shortcut; choose Properties, Shortcut and edit the Start In field to the desktop path (`c:\winnt\profiles\username\desktop` for Windows NT or `c:\documents and settings\username\desktop` for Windows 2000).

TIP Saved GroupWise messages (DOC files) are best used by the GroupWise client to retrieve the message contents into a new mail message. To do this, open a new mail message and click File, Retrieve and select the saved message file. The contents are added to the new mail message. This is very handy for frequently used communications, such as a weekly corporate email. Because the extension of saved messages is .doc, you can also open them into Microsoft Word, edit the email messages, save them back to the disk, and retrieve them into GroupWise, as discussed.

Printing Messages

The Print option under the File menu enables you to specify custom print settings. To select paper type, fonts, and other options, follow these steps:

1. Click the File menu.

2. Choose Print.

3. Choose Properties. Click the Page Setup button.

4. The dialog box shown in Figure 5.19 appears. Select the desired tab, set the options you want, and click OK.

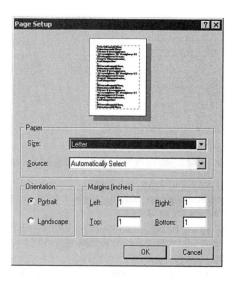

FIGURE 5.19
You set up your printer's options using this dialog box.

NOTE The Page Setup dialog box is unique for each type of printer you have installed.

To print messages, follow these steps:

1. Select the messages you want to print.
2. Choose Print from the File menu (or press Ctrl+P).
3. Select either the message or the attachment you would like to print.
4. Click the Print button.

NOTE The Print Attachment with Associated Application option launches the application associated with the file attachment and prints the attachment from that application. Use this option if you want to preserve the formatting of the file attachment.

Using the Checklist

One of the most convenient new features of GroupWise 6.5 is the Checklist. In previous versions of GroupWise, the Task List folder simply contained every task that was in a mailbox, displayed in a list fashion. To place an item into the Task List folder, you had to change the message type to Task.

The GroupWise 6.5 Checklist allows you to simply place any message—using click and drag—into the Checklist folder for action at some point.

NOTE The message retains its original type and does not become a task. Tasks are not contained in the Checklist folder unless placed there on purpose.

Figure 5.20 shows messages in the Checklist folder.

Once a message is placed into the Checklist folder, a box is displayed next to the item, allowing it to be "completed" by a single mouse click.

To move items into the Checklist folder, select the message (or messages) with a single mouse click (or Ctrl+click or Shift+click to select multiple messages) and drag them to the Checklist folder.

NOTE To keep a copy of the message in its original folder, hold the Ctrl key down while performing the click-and-drag steps.

CHAPTER 5 Message Management

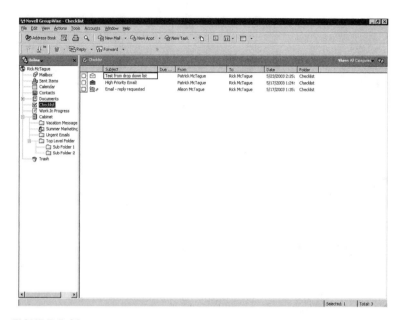

FIGURE 5.20
The Checklist folder contains messages requiring some type of action.

Optionally, you can select messages as described, right-click, and choose Move to Checklist Folder from the QuickMenu.

TIP You can view items in any folder as "Checklist" items. That way, you can work within the same folder. With any folder selected, choose View, Display Settings, As Checklist. To make this change permanent on a particular folder, right-click the folder, click Properties, click the Display tab, choose Checklist under the View By drop-down list, and click OK.

Using Categories

Another powerful new feature of GroupWise 6.5 is *categories*. You can create unlimited color-coded categories for your messages based on anything you would like. There are four default categories to get you started: Follow-up, Low Priority, Personal, and Urgent. You could make a category for a project you are working on, assign a color to it, and be able to quickly tell if any message pertains to that project.

To assign a message or group of messages to a category, select a message with a single mouse click (or Ctrl+click or Shift+click to select multiple messages), right-click, and select the category from the pop-up list of categories to the side of the QuickMenu when you move the mouse to Categories. Optionally, you can select Categories from the Actions menu.

To create additional categories, select Categories from the Actions menu and choose More. You will see the dialog box show in Figure 5.21.

FIGURE 5.21
The Categories dialog box lets you create and customize your own categories.

At the bottom of this dialog box, enter the name of the category you would like to create and then click Add. To change the color associated with any category, select the category, choose Edit Color, select your new color from the palette, and click OK.

From this same dialog box you can rename or delete a category; the "primary category" is the color that will display on an item with more than one category associated to it. For example, if you have associated Urgent and New Project to the same item, and Urgent is set as the primary category, the item will be displayed in red in the folder (if red denotes the Urgent category).

Managing Outgoing Messages

The Sent Items folder is a Find folder that automatically searches for all messages you have sent, regardless of the personal folder you filed them in. You retain access to these messages for three purposes: to track the status of the messages, to edit and resend the messages, and to retract the messages.

Checking the Status of Sent Items

GroupWise offers the distinctive feature of tracking the status of sent messages. With status types, you can find out the disposition of any message you have sent.

You can get some information about the message simply by looking at the icon to the left of the message in the Sent Items folder. For example, if the item has not been opened by the recipient, the envelope is closed. If the recipient has opened the message, the envelope icon is open.

The status information in GroupWise corresponds to specific message types. For example, you can check to see if a Phone message has been read or if a task you sent has been completed. However, you can't see if an email message has been completed because you can only mark a task completed. Table 5.3 lists the different status types, and Table 5.4 shows how they correspond to each message type.

TABLE 5.3 Description of Status Messages

STATUS	DESCRIPTION
Delivered	The message has been delivered to the recipient's Mailbox.
Replied	The message has been replied to by the recipient.
Opened	The message has been opened by the recipient.
Retracted	The message has been retracted from the recipient's Mailbox.
Deleted	The message has been moved to the recipient's Trash.
Emptied	The message has been purged from the recipient's Trash.
Completed	The task has been completed.
Accepted	The appointment, note, or task has been accepted by the recipient.
Declined	The appointment, note, or task has been declined by the recipient.
Downloaded	The message has been downloaded by a remote client.
Transferred	The message has been transferred to the gateway.

NOTE The only status information you can obtain about a message sent outside of your GroupWise system (such as an email message sent to the Internet) is Transferred. You can get a return notification email when "All" status is selected and the email is sent to a receiving system that supports mail delivery notification.

TABLE 5.4 Message Type/Status Information Correlation

STATUS	EMAIL MESSAGE	PHONE MESSAGE	MEETING REQUEST	TASK ASSIGNMENT	REMINDER NOTE
Delivered	X	X	X	X	X
Replied	X	X	X	X	X
Opened	X	X	X	X	X
Retracted	X	X	X	X	X
Deleted	X	X	X	X	X
Emptied	X	X	X	X	X
Completed				X	
Accepted			X	X	X
Declined			X	X	X
Downloaded	X	X	X	X	X
Transferred	X	X	X	X	X

To check the status of a message, follow these steps:

1. Click the Sent Items folder.

2. Double-click the message for which you want the status and choose Properties. (Alternatively, you can select a message, right-click it, and choose Properties from the QuickMenu.)

TIP The default for double-clicking a message in the Sent Items folder is set the first time you run GroupWise and double-click the item. You are prompted to either view the properties or open the message. To change this, select Options on the Tools menu, double-click Environment, and select the Default Actions tab. Sent Items default actions are in the upper-left corner.

Figure 5.22 shows a typical message with status properties.

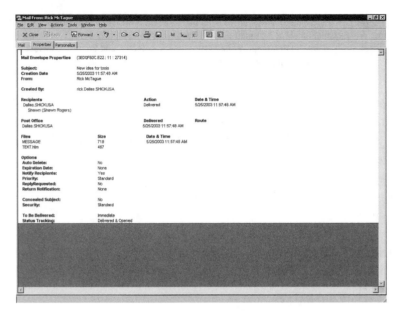

FIGURE 5.22
The properties of a sent message display delivery information.

Retracting Messages

Retracting a message is extremely useful if you have regrets about a sent message or if you have any other reason to recall a message you have sent. As long as the message has not been opened, you can retract it.

> **NOTE** You cannot retract messages sent through a gateway to another mail system, such as messages you send to Internet users. You can only retract a message through a gateway if the recipient's system is GroupWise.

To retract a message, follow these steps:

1. Click the Sent Items folder.

2. Click the message you want to retract and press the Delete key, or choose Edit and then Delete. (As a shortcut, right-click a message and choose Delete from the QuickMenu.)

3. From the Delete Item dialog box, shown in Figure 5.23, make a choice about which Mailboxes you want to remove the message from:

▶ **My Mailbox**—Removes the message from your Sent Items folder only, leaving a copy in the recipient's Mailbox

▶ **Recipient's Mailbox**—Removes the message from all recipients' Mailboxes, leaving a copy in your Sent Items folder

▶ **All Mailboxes**—Removes the message from all recipients' Mailboxes as well as from your Sent Items folder

NOTE If you are using GroupWise in remote mode (discussed in Chapter 10, "Remote Access"), you see an additional option: Delete from Master and Remote Mailbox.

4. Click OK and the message is retracted.

FIGURE 5.23
The Delete Item dialog box lets you determine the options for the retraction of a message.

NOTE You can only retract a message if the recipient has not opened it. The Delete from Recipient's Mailbox option is the safest way to retract because you still keep a copy of the item in your Sent Items folder (for status tracking, resending, and so on).

Resending Messages

If you have ever sent a message to the president of your company, only to read it later and find a glaring typo, or you forgot to attach the file you were going to send, you should appreciate being able to resend messages with GroupWise. From the Sent Items folder, you can edit a message you have sent and resend it—with an option to retract the original message.

To resend a message, follow these steps:

1. Click the Sent Items folder.

2. Click the message you want to edit, choose Actions, and select Resend. (As a shortcut, right-click a message and choose Resend from the QuickMenu.)

3. Edit the message, click the Send button, and answer Yes when you are prompted with the question, Retract Original Item? (see Figure 5.24).

FIGURE 5.24
When you resend a message, you'll see the Resend dialog box, which allows you to remove the old message from the recipients' Mailboxes.

Managing the Trash

Do you know someone who likes to keep every possession, supposing that someday he might "need" it, only to clutter up an attic or basement? Well, GroupWise is like that. Deleted messages stick around in the Trash folder until you manually empty it, or until trash day rolls around. Trash day is set up just like it is in your neighborhood—once a week. However, you can change the default setting for emptying the Trash folder. (We explain how to change the default setting in Chapter 11.)

You saw how to delete messages in Chapter 3, "Messaging Fundamentals." Once messages have been deleted, you can perform one of two actions: undelete the messages or purge them from the Trash.

Here's how to undelete a message:

1. Highlight the Trash folder. All deleted items appear in the Items Area.

2. Select a message or group of messages from the Items Area.

3. Select Edit and Undelete. (Alternatively, right-click the message or group and choose Undelete from the QuickMenu.)

The message returns to its original location.

To purge the Trash, simply choose Edit, Empty Trash.

Summary

In this chapter we discussed the features of GroupWise that enable you to organize, find, sort, and manage the messages you receive. With the incredible increase of email and its many uses, GroupWise provides these features to allow you to build complex searches for messages meeting certain criteria, to share folders with your co-workers, and to track the status of the messages you send. In Chapter 6, "Personal Calendaring and Task Management," we will look into managing your time using the personal calendaring aspects of GroupWise.

CHAPTER 6

Personal Calendaring and Task Management

In this chapter we show you how to use GroupWise 6.5 to replace your old-fashioned calendar or daily planner. The time-management features of GroupWise are extraordinarily useful; once you start using these features, you'll wonder how you ever got by without them.

When you showed up for work this morning and turned on your computer, one of the first things you probably did was check your email. After that, you likely checked your calendar to see what appointments you had for the day. With GroupWise, the integration of the email interface with the Calendar system makes it very easy to do most of your communications and scheduling with one program. As you saw in Chapter 1, "Introduction to GroupWise 6.5," switching from email to the Calendar is as simple as clicking the Calendar folder.

With the Calendar's built-in views, you can instantly display Calendar items, such as appointments and tasks. Later in this chapter you'll learn how to change your view to one that suits your needs.

To use the GroupWise Calendar system most effectively, you need to understand the difference between the various Calendar items. The Calendar keeps track of three different kinds of personal reminders: posted appointments, posted reminder notes, and posted tasks.

Table 6.1 explains the different Calendar items.

TABLE 6.1 GroupWise 6.5 Calendar Items

ITEM	DESCRIPTION
Posted appointments	Personal meetings and events on a certain date with a start time and an end time (duration)
Posted reminder notes	Personal reminders for a certain date
Posted tasks	Personal task entries that appear as check box entries in your Calendar from the start date through the due date, with a priority level

Note the distinction between personal Calendar items (posted) and group Calendar items. Posted items are not sent to anyone; you post them to your own Calendar. Group items are sent to other people in much the same way you send email messages. Group calendaring is discussed in Chapter 7, "Group Calendaring and Task Management."

Using the Calendar Interface

When you click the Calendar folder, a default view of your GroupWise Calendar appears in the right side of the main GroupWise screen, as shown in Figure 6.1.

New to GroupWise 6.5 is the Categories feature. This feature lets you group and organize the various GroupWise message types in categories of your choosing. For example, you might create categories called Work, Personal, and Family. Depending on your current activity, you might want only messages that fall into a particular category to display. The category selector is located in the status bar at the top right of the GroupWise Calendar display.

Below the status bar is another row that contains several Calendar control buttons. The date selector displays the current date. The button next to the date selector displays a pop-up display of the current month. The button with the sun icon returns your Calendar display to the current day (today). The number buttons let you quickly advance your Calendar view by 1 day, 7 days, 1 month, or 1 year.

Advance to date buttons   Status bar
Today button   View selection buttons

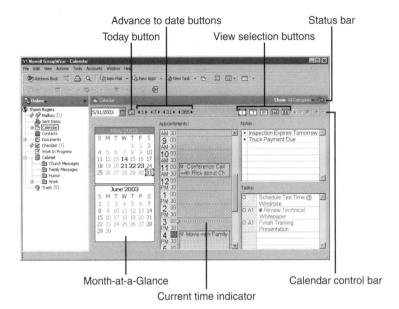

Month-at-a-Glance   Calendar control bar
Current time indicator

FIGURE 6.1
The GroupWise Calendar helps you manage your appointments, tasks, and notes.

By default, five numbered buttons appear at the top-right corner of the Calendar display. These buttons allow you to quickly display your favorite view of your Calendar information. If you place your mouse over each button, a pop-up explanation will display that indicates either Day, Week, Month, Year, or Multi-User view. (Multi-User view allows you to view calendars of other GroupWise users who have granted you "proxy" access. Proxy access is explained in Chapter 8, "Advanced Features.")

To the right of the view buttons are five more buttons that are not active in the default Calendar view. These buttons are used in other Calendar views to display items types that are not displayed in different views. For example, in the Week view, tasks are not displayed by default. You can click the check box to open a display of your tasks.

NOTE All your Calendar items—both personal and group—appear in your Calendar. This chapter discusses personal items only. Chapter 7 discusses group items.

TIP You can change the function of the view buttons by right-clicking any of the buttons and choosing Properties. You can edit the buttons, change the order in which they appear, add new ones, or delete the buttons you don't use in the Calendar folder.

Day View

The Day view (shown previously in Figure 6.1) displays your appointments, reminder notes, and tasks in separate panes in the Items Area along with multiple months (2 to 4 months usually, depending on your computer's resolution and the size of the GroupWise window). The subject line of each Calendar item appears. To see the details of an item in the Day view, simply double-click the heading bar button (Appointments, Reminder Notes, or Tasks) for the item.

TIP If you have enabled the QuickViewer, the message contents of each Calendar item will appear in the QuickViewer pane at the bottom of the screen.

Notice that the current (approximate) time is displayed in the Appointments field with a small clock icon and a dashed line.

TIP You can quickly adjust the duration of a posted appointment by clicking and dragging the appointment border.

Week View

The Week view displays your Calendar items for several consecutive days, as shown in Figure 6.2.

You can add or subtract days from the view by clicking the plus (+) or minus (−) sign in the top-right corner of the display. (The maximum number of days/weeks you can see depends on your computer's resolution and the size of the GroupWise window.) You can also navigate forward in the calendar by clicking the right arrows to move ahead or the left arrows to move back. You can also click the Appointments, Reminder Notes, or Tasks button to determine whether these items are displayed.

TIP Leave your mouse pointer over a Calendar item to see a quick view of the details of the item, or you can double-click the item to open the full appointment.

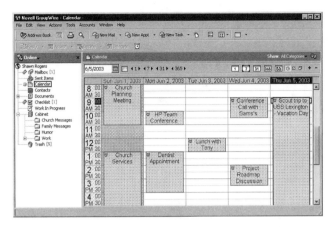

FIGURE 6.2
The Week view displays your appointments for several consecutive days.

Month View

The Month view displays your Calendar items for the entire month, as shown in Figure 6.3. You can use the arrows at the top of the display to change the month. You can use the Appointments, Reminder Notes, and Tasks buttons to change what information is displayed in the Month view.

> **TIP** Right-click any day to create a new Calendar item quickly. You can also double-click any day to see a larger display for that date.

Year View

The Year view shows an entire year's worth of items, as shown in Figure 6.4. Note that days in boldface are days for which you have Calendar items set. You can use the arrows next to the year to change the year being displayed.

> **TIP** Double-click any day in the Year view to see details about that day.

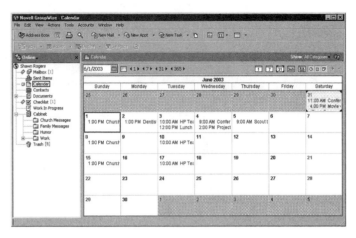

FIGURE 6.3
The Month view lets you see an entire month's appointments in a single window.

FIGURE 6.4
The Year view lets you see your entire year calendar at a glance.

Multi-User View

The Multi-User view is used to view more than one person's calendar information at a time. We cover the Multi-User calendar in Chapter 7.

Changing Dates and Views

From any of these views, if you want to see the Calendar items for a different day, click the calendar icon in the upper left of the Calendar view and go to the date you want to see. You can also select View, Go to Date from the drop-down menu.

To return to the current day's Calendar items quickly, click the Go to Today button (the one with the sun on it) or select View, Go to Today from the drop-down menu.

In addition to the Calendar folder views previously discussed, you can choose from 15 different views of the Calendar, which are available from the Window, Calendar drop-down menu. These views open the Calendar in its own window, separate from the main GroupWise view. These views are listed in Table 6.2. You'll want to experiment with them until you find the one that best suits your work style.

TIP You can add any of the alternate Calendar views to the Calendar folder buttons at the top right of the Calendar view by right-clicking any of the buttons, choosing Properties, selecting New, picking your view from the drop-down list, giving the view a name, and then clicking OK.

TABLE 6.2 Calendar Views Available from the Drop-Down Menu

NAME	FEATURES
Day	Displays appointments, reminder notes, and tasks for a single day. Monthly calendars are displayed to quickly move to a specific date.
Week	Displays appointments several days at a time. You can also view tasks and reminders with the control buttons.
Week & Calendar	Displays appointments, reminder notes, and tasks 5 to 7 days at a time, with month at a glance.
Month	Displays appointments, reminder notes, and tasks a month at a time.
Month & Calendar	Displays appointments, reminder notes, and tasks a month at a time, with several months at a glance.
Year	Displays the entire year. Boldface dates on the calendar contain scheduled items.
Desk Calendar	Displays daily appointments and tasks 1 month at a time.

TABLE 6.2 Continued

NAME	FEATURES
Notebook	Displays reminder notes and tasks for 1 day.
Day Projects	Displays expanded Cabinet folders, group appointments, tasks, and reminder notes, with multiple months at a glance.
Day Planner	Displays tasks, appointments, and reminder notes, with multiple months at a glance.
Project Planner	Displays tasks and reminder notes, with all folders expanded and multiple months at a glance, as shown in Figure 6.5.
Appt (sm)	Displays appointments for 1 day.
Note (sm)	Displays reminder notes for 1 day.
Task (sm)	Displays tasks for 1 day.
Multi-User	Displays appointments, reminder notes, and tasks for multiple users.

FIGURE 6.5
The Project Planner view is 1 of 15 optional Calendar views available from the drop-down menu.

To open a Calendar view, click Window, Calendar and then select the view from the list. Alternatively, you can click on the drop-down arrow next to the Calendar button on the toolbar.

TIP Once you have found a view that you like, you can set it as the default by selecting Tools, Options, Environment, Views. (Setting default options and customizing the Toolbar are explained in Chapter 10, "Remote Access.")

Task List

In previous versions of GroupWise, the Task List was a system folder in the main GroupWise screen. In GroupWise 6.5, the Task List folder has been replaced with the Checklist folder, which is more comprehensive and functional than the former Task List folder.

However, the various Calendar views provide you with a comprehensive list of the tasks that you have created or received. You can move a task to the Checklist folder by simply clicking and dragging it from the Calendar view to the Checklist folder.

NOTE Any type of GroupWise message can be placed into the Checklist folder. When a message is placed in the Checklist folder, it has a new task-focused tab when you open it. The Checklist tab in the message lets you prioritize the item and assign it a due date.

The Checklist folder is very useful for storing email messages you have received that require a follow-up action. The Checklist folder was explained in more detail in Chapter 5, "Message Management."

Making Posted Appointments

A large part of time management involves scheduling appointments, and GroupWise provides an easy-to-use interface for creating and managing your personal engagements. Posted appointment messages only appear on your Calendar; you don't send them to other people. Figure 6.6 shows an example of a posted appointment.

As you can see in Figure 6.6, a posted appointment includes the following information: appointment date, start time, duration, and place. The time increment (default of 15 minutes) can be changed, as well as the date format. You can customize GroupWise to use military date and time as well as other formats. (See Chapter 10 for more information on customizing your GroupWise environment.) The Subject line of an appointment appears in the Calendar.

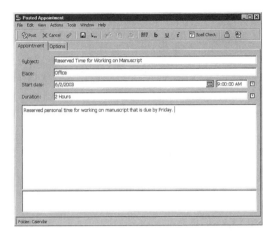

FIGURE 6.6
The Posted Appointment screen lets you manage your personal appointments.

TIP One of the best uses for a "personal" posted appointment is to block out time on your own schedule that will show as "busy" when other individuals look at your schedule or do a "busy" search to try to schedule a meeting. This allows you to clear a portion of your schedule to work on projects that require distraction-free efforts.

To create a posted appointment, follow these steps:

1. Click the down arrow next to the New Appt button on the Toolbar and choose Posted Appointment from the list. Alternatively, in the Calendar view, double-click the time for which you want to make the posted appointment, and you will achieve the same result.

TIP If your Calendar folder is open, you can also click the start time in the Appointments field, drag the mouse pointer to the end time of the appointment, release the mouse button, and simply start typing the subject of the posted appointment. Using this method, the appointment's subject line will also be the same text as the message body.

2. Enter a subject for the appointment and place more detailed information in the message area.

3. Fill in the appointment's date, start time, and duration, and choose Post to add the appointment to your Calendar.

You can also set alarms for your appointments. Here's how to set an alarm:

1. Right-click an appointment in your Calendar view.

2. Choose Alarm from the QuickMenu. The Set Alarm dialog box will display.

3. Specify, in hours and minutes, how much advance notice you want. The maximum is 99 hours and 59 minutes. You can also set up a variety of sounds for the alarm. (See Chapter 10 for information on how to customize the alarm.)

4. Click SET. Notice the alarm clock icon next to the Appointment.

NOTE Once you set an alarm, you can change the time or remove the alarm by right-clicking the appointment, selecting Alarms, and then clicking the Clear button.

Creating Posted Tasks

Posted tasks are very useful, reminding you to finish assignments or projects that may last for several days. Your posted tasks appear in the Tasks field in your Calendar views.

NOTE If you want a task to appear in your Checklist folder, you need to either create the posted task with the Checklist folder active (selected) or click and drag the task from the Calendar view's Tasks field into the Checklist folder.

Each task has a start date, an end date, and a priority level, as shown in Figure 6.7. The priority level determines the order in which tasks appear in the list, based on an alphabetic and numeric code. For example, a task with a priority of A1 appears before A2, and A2 appears before B1. The code you assign to a task is completely up to you. You can use only letters or only numbers if you prefer.

The Subject line of each task you create appears on the starting day's Calendar and will carry forward each day until you mark the Task Completed check box. If a task is not marked completed by the due date, it will continue to be carried forward, but it will appear red in the Task List.

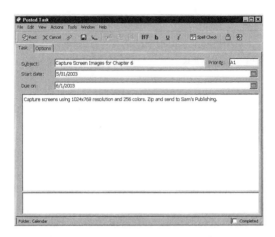

FIGURE 6.7
The Posted Task screen lets you manage your personal "to-do" list.

To create a posted task, follow these steps:

1. Click the arrow next to the New Task button on the Toolbar and choose Posted Task from the list.

TIP You can also double-click in the Task Area of your Calendar to create a new posted task.

---

2. Enter a subject for the task. You can place more detailed information in the message area.

3. Enter a priority level for the task (or leave the priority setting blank if you like).

4. Enter a start date (which must be today's date or later) and then enter an end date in the Due on field.

5. Click Post to enter the task in your Calendar.

To mark a task completed, click the Task heading button in the Calendar folder. Click the box next to the task in the Task List. Notice that a check mark appears in the box.

Posting Reminder Notes

Reminder notes can be added to your Calendar and linked to certain dates, as shown in Figure 6.8. The Subject line of each note appears in your Calendar view. You can use reminder notes to remind yourself about anything you like—for example, picking up your dry cleaning. You might also use a recurring note to mark paydays on your Calendar.

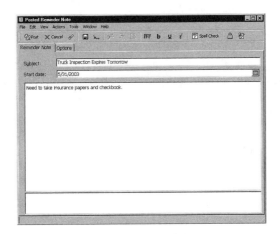

FIGURE 6.8
The Posted Reminder Note screen lets you link a reminder to a specific date.

To create a reminder note, follow these steps:

1. Double-click the Note pane under your appointments.

TIP If your Calendar folder is open, simply click an empty line in the Reminder Note box and start typing the subject of your note. Click elsewhere to enter the note into your Calendar.

---

2. Enter a subject for the note. If you like, you can place details about the note in the message area.

3. Fill in the date for the note and click POST to add the note to your Calendar.

Remember, reminder notes will not carry from one date to the next. Reminders are specific to the day for which they were created.

Rescheduling Appointments, Tasks, and Reminder Notes

Rescheduling a posted appointment, task, or reminder note only requires a simple click and drag of the mouse. Here's how to move an appointment, task, or reminder note to a different day:

1. Open your Calendar folder.

2. If the day you need to move the item to does not appear, use either the Week or Month button on the Calendar folder view, or open the Day view of the Calendar. (See the "Using the Calendar Interface" section at the beginning of this chapter for instructions on changing views.) The Day view displays multiple months at a glance.

3. Click the appointment, task, or reminder note you want to reschedule and drag it to the new day.

To change the time of a posted appointment, follow these steps:

1. Open your Calendar folder and single-click the appointment you want to change.

2. With the mouse button held down, drag the appointment to a new time on the same day, and the appointment will move.

The preceding steps show you how to move a posted appointment, task, or reminder note from one day to another. You can also *copy* a posted appointment from one day to another by holding the Ctrl key as you click and drag the posted appointment from the current date to another date.

Changing Calendar Item Types

Suppose you are over halfway finished with a new posted appointment, only to realize that you should be making a posted task instead. Instead of canceling and starting over, you can change one message type into another, on the fly. For example, you can keep all the information about the appointment (subject, message body, and so on) and change it into a new task, retaining all the information.

There are two ways to change a Calendar item from one type to another. The first method is best to use after the item has been created: Simply click the Calendar item and drag it to another area in the Calendar display. For example, you could click a posted appointment and drag it to the Task Area, and the item will change to a Posted Task. The second method is best to use while the item is being created: Anytime you create a new Calendar item, click the Change Item Type button on the Toolbar (it has an arrow with two dots). Then click the desired new Calendar item type and choose OK. The screen will change to the new item type.

NOTE Notice that when you use the first method, the mouse pointer changes to represent what you are doing, using the item icons with an arrow in between.

TIP You can also use the Edit, Change To menu option to change the item type.

Summary

In this chapter you have seen the many features of GroupWise as they relate to your own calendar. The posted appointments, reminder notes, and tasks that you create to manage your time can also be used to invite people to meetings, remind them of events on a certain day, and to delegate tasks. The next chapter shows you how to make the most of the GroupWise 6.5 group scheduling and workflow features.

Group Calendaring and Task Management

In Chapter 6, "Personal Calendaring and Task Management," you learned how to manage your personal Calendar items, such as appointments and tasks. In this chapter we show you how to use the GroupWise 6.5 workgroup and collaboration features, including group calendaring and task management.

Scheduling Meetings

When you want to schedule a meeting with other people, you send an appointment message.

> **NOTE** Appointment messages that you send to other people are sometimes referred to as *meetings* or *meeting requests*.

In some cases you may need to schedule a meeting for someone else, such as your supervisor. GroupWise enables you to schedule meetings for others (in other words, meetings that you don't plan to attend).

You can use the GroupWise Proxy feature to view and manage others' Calendars. (Chapter 8, "Advanced Features," explains the Proxy feature.)

Sending Appointments

You send appointments to other GroupWise users to schedule meetings —either for yourself or for someone else. When you want to send an appointment, you must set a start date, a start time, and a duration—just like you do for posted (personal) appointments. The only difference is that you are sending the appointment request to others, not just adding the appointment to your Calendar.

To create and send an appointment, follow these steps:

1. Click File, New, Appointment or click the New Appt button on the Toolbar. You'll see the screen shown in Figure 7.1.

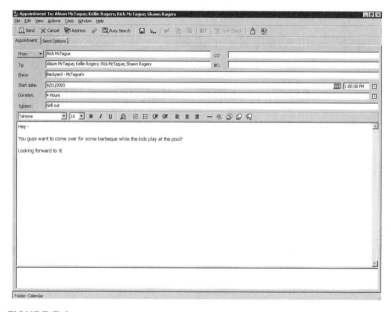

FIGURE 7.1
The New Appointment screen provides many fields to designate details about the meeting, such as place and duration.

2. Address the appointment message just as you would any other type of GroupWise message—by entering the names in the To field or by using the Address Book. If you plan to attend the meeting, make sure you include your own name in the To field. If you do not include your own name, the appointment will not appear in your Calendar. (By default, GroupWise inserts your name in the To field when you create an appointment.)

3. Enter the location of the meeting in the Place field.

> **TIP** If your system administrator has made the meeting place (for example, a certain conference room) a resource, you can schedule the room at the same time you send the appointment. Open the Address Book and click View, Filter for Resources. Select the room from the list of resources. If the room has not been defined as a resource, you can describe the meeting place in the Place field, but the room will not be reserved by GroupWise.

4. Enter a subject in the Subject line. (Be descriptive because only the Subject line appears in the recipients' Calendars.)

5. Enter detailed information about the meeting in the Message field. If you like, you can attach a file, such as the meeting agenda.

6. Set the date of the meeting by typing the date in the Start Date field or by clicking the small calendar icon to the right of that field.

> **NOTE** If you want to create a recurring appointment, you can use the Auto-Date feature, explained later in this chapter.

7. Set the time of the meeting by typing the time in the field to the right of the small calendar icon or by clicking the small clock icon next to that field.

8. Enter the duration of the meeting in the Duration field (or set the duration by clicking the small clock icon to the right of the Duration field).

9. Choose Send.

The appointment appears in the recipients' Mailboxes and Calendars.

When you schedule meetings, you can use the Busy Search feature to find a time when all attendees are available. The Busy Search feature automatically sets the date, time, and duration of the meeting. Busy Searches are explained in the next section.

Busy Search

The Busy Search feature is a very powerful GroupWise scheduling tool. You no longer need to call people in advance of a meeting to find a time when everyone can meet. GroupWise takes care of that chore for you.

To perform a Busy Search when scheduling a meeting, follow these steps:

1. Open a new appointment message and use the Address Book to place the attendees' addresses in the To field.

2. Click the Busy Search button in the Toolbar. GroupWise searches the users' Calendars and displays the Choose Appointment Time dialog box, as shown in Figure 7.2.

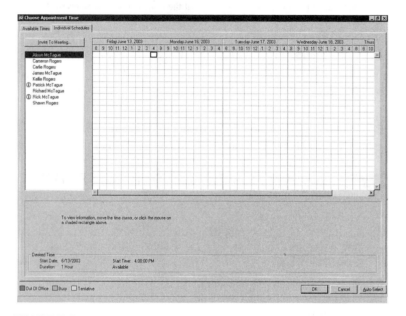

FIGURE 7.2
Busy Search will display the availability for invitees to your meeting.

The Choose Appointment Time dialog box presents you with a grid showing you the schedule of each user you specified. An empty space across from the username indicates that the user is available for that time.

If you want GroupWise to show you the times when all users are available, click the Available Times tab (see Figure 7.3).

You can select the appointment time from either of the Choose Appointment Time screens. To set the appointment time, follow these steps:

1. Click the highlighted box in the grid and drag it to a time the attendees are available. You can click and drag the sides of this box to increase or decrease the duration of the meeting.

2. Click OK. The date and time of the meeting appear in the appropriate fields of the appointment message.

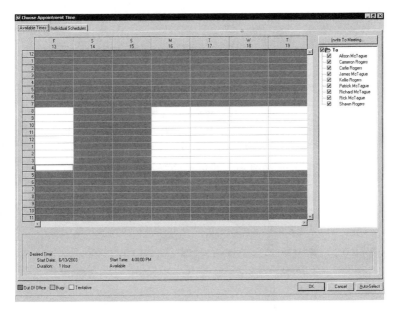

FIGURE 7.3
The Available Times tab will help you select the best time for the meeting.

Here are some handy Busy Search tips:

▶ To include more users in the Busy Search from the Choose Appointment Time dialog box, click the Invite To Meeting button.

▶ If there isn't a time when all attendees are free, you can extend the search to include more days by clicking the Invite To Meeting button and increasing the value in the Number Of Days To Search field.

▶ When the Choose Appointment Time dialog box shows that some users are busy, you can find out what a user has scheduled by clicking the box representing that timeslot. (You can see the person's schedule only if the user has granted you access rights to his or her Calendar.)

▶ The Auto-Select button selects a time when all the selected users are free for the duration you have specified.

▶ You can exclude a user from the Busy Search without removing the user from the To field by choosing the Available Times tab and then clearing the check mark that appears next to the user's name in the right side of the dialog box. (This exclusion feature is useful when someone should be invited, but it is not absolutely necessary for that person to attend.)

► To perform a Busy Search before creating your appointment message, choose Tools, Busy Search. Enter the users in the dialog box that appears.

► You can add names to the Busy Search by clicking the Invite To Meeting button. You can delete names from the Busy Search by clicking the username and pressing the Delete key.

► If you are Busy Searching for multiple users, GroupWise may take awhile to return the results on all users. You can minimize the Busy Search dialog box and work on other tasks while GroupWise receives the Busy Search results. A status box will appear on your Windows taskbar showing you the search progress.

► You can do a Busy Search for a resource (such as a conference room, company car, or VCR) to find out times when the resource is not reserved.

Here's how to change Busy Search defaults:

1. Click Tools, Options.

2. Double-click the Date and Time icon.

3. Choose the Busy Search tab.

NOTE The Busy Search feature is only useful if all GroupWise users keep their Calendars up to date. Remember also that appointments can be delegated by recipients. Check the status of the message to see if any of the intended attendees have delegated the appointment to another person.

Busy Search is a very good tool to make sure the meetings you are scheduling work with the schedules of the attendees.

iCal Appointments

iCal is a relatively new standard for calendar information sent to Internet recipients.

When you are sending a new appointment to an Internet recipient and that person's system can work with iCal messages, the appointment will be displayed in his or her native system's calendar.

NOTE In GroupWise 6.5, this feature only works if you are sending appointments from POP3/IMAP4 accounts (discussed in Chapter 8).

To enable iCal appointments, verify that you are in either Caching or Remote mode and then click Accounts, Account Options, General Options. Select the option Use iCal when Sending Appointments via SMTP and then click OK.

Sending Tasks

Use GroupWise task messages for assigning projects to other GroupWise users. Tasks are also useful for large projects that involve many people.

To send a task, follow these steps:

1. Choose File, New, Task or click the New Task button on the Toolbar. The task message screen shown in Figure 7.4 appears.

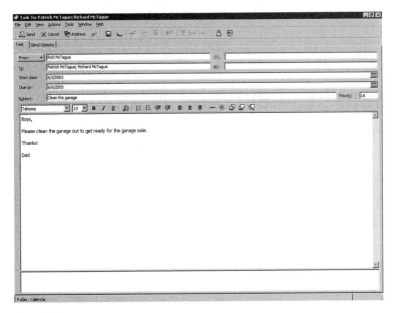

FIGURE 7.4
A task can be delegated to another GroupWise user.

2. Address the task message by typing in the recipient's name or by using the Address Book.

3. Enter a priority code for the task. The task priority can be a character, a number, or a character followed by a number. For example, valid priority codes include A, B, C, 1, 2, 3, A1, B1, B2, and so on.

4. Enter the subject and message in the appropriate fields.

5. Select a start date. The start date is the date when the task will first appear in the recipient's Calendar, after the recipient accepts the task from his or her Mailbox.

6. Select a due date. Tasks that are not completed before the due date turn red in the recipient's Calendar.

7. Choose Send.

In addition to the priority code you enter in the task message screen, you can also set a priority for the task itself. Here's how:

1. While you are composing a new task message, choose the Send Options tab.

2. Select High, Standard, or Low priority.

3. Click Send.

Sending tasks allows you to electronically delegate activities to co-workers.

Sending Reminder Notes

Use reminder notes to send reminders to people. Reminder notes are very useful as meeting reminders because notes appear on specific days in the recipients' Calendars. Often, notes are used to remind others about specific assignments for upcoming meetings.

To send a reminder note, follow these steps:

1. Select File, New, Reminder Note.

2. Enter the information in the To, Subject, and Message fields.

3. Specify a date for the note in the Start date field.

4. Click Send.

Figure 7.5 shows a typical reminder note.

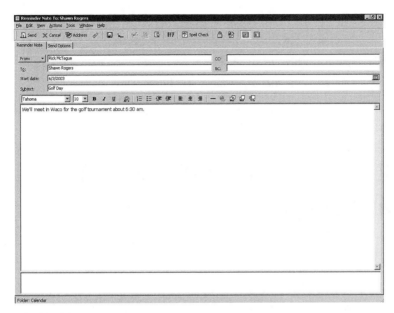

FIGURE 7.5
A reminder note can be sent to other users for items that pertain to a particular date, such as payday reminders.

As you can see, reminder notes add items to your calendar to track daily activities.

Monitoring Appointments, Tasks, and Notes

Users often fail to keep their Calendars up to date, and even though a Busy Search may show that they are available, they may not be. After you send an appointment, you should monitor the status of the message to find out whether it has been accepted, declined, or delegated (or simply ignored).

If a recipient has declined the message and has provided a comment explaining why, that comment appears in the message status information, not as a message in your Mailbox. (See Chapter 5, "Message Management," for more information on checking the status of sent items.)

To see whether the recipients have accepted, declined, or delegated a message, and to view their comments, follow these steps:

1. Open your Sent Items folder.

2. Right-click the message and choose Properties.

You can use these steps to see whether users have accepted, declined, or completed the items you have invited them to and delegated to them.

Retracting Appointments, Tasks, and Notes

Unlike regular email messages, you can retract appointments, tasks, and notes after the recipients have opened them. When you retract an appointment, task, or note, it is removed from the recipients' Calendars and Mailboxes.

To retract an appointment, task, or note, follow these steps:

1. Open your Sent Items folder and highlight the message to be retracted.

2. Press the Delete key (or right-click the message and select Delete).

3. Select Recipient's Mailbox or All Mailboxes and then click OK.

Here's how to reschedule or resend a Calendar entry:

1. Right-click the message in the Sent Items folder and select Resend.

2. Change the message information, if necessary, and click Send.

3. If you want to retract the original entry, choose Yes when prompted.

4. Because the recipients receive no warning (the item simply disappears from their Calendars), it is good messaging etiquette to let them know you have retracted the item.

The ability to retract items you send allows you to "take back" or edit these items.

Acting on Received Appointments, Tasks, and Notes

The appointments, tasks, and notes you receive from other GroupWise users appear in your Mailbox along with other email messages. Appointments, tasks, and notes also appear in your Calendar folder or in your Calendar view on the specified date. In the Calendar they appear in italics until you accept them, indicating that these items are tentative and have not been accepted.

Figure 7.6 shows an opened Calendar folder with accepted and unaccepted appointments, tasks, and notes.

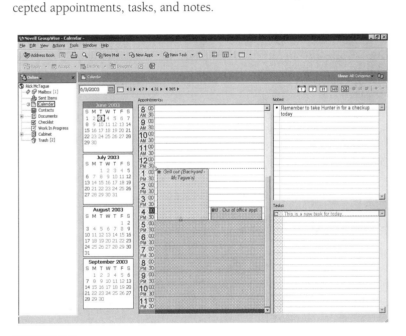

FIGURE 7.6
Unaccepted Calendar items will be displayed in italics until you accept or decline them.

You have several options when you receive an appointment, task, or note from someone else. You can accept the entry, and it will convert the tentative (italicized) entry to a regular (nonitalicized) entry. Alternatively, you can decline the message, and it will move to your Trash folder.

Accepting

To accept an appointment, task, or note from the Mailbox or Calendar folder, double-click the icon to open it and choose the Accept button. Alternatively, you can right-click the item and choose Accept from the QuickMenu.

The Accept With Options dialog box will appear, which enables you to send a comment to the sender of the message. This comment will appear in the sender's message properties.

Either at the time of acceptance, or even after the appointment has been accepted, you can change how the item is displayed in your Calendar. Free, Busy, Tentative, and Out of Office are the options that display as different color shadings in the Calendar.

To change how an appointment is displayed in your Calendar, right-click the appointment, choose Show Appointment As, and select an option.

Declining

To decline an appointment, task, or note from the Mailbox or Calendar folder, double-click the icon to open it and choose the Decline button (or right-click the item and choose Decline from the QuickMenu). When you decline an entry, you are given the option to comment about why you have declined. If you enter a comment, the sender can see it when he or she checks the status of the message you declined.

Delegating

If you receive an appointment that you cannot attend or a task you cannot complete, but you desire that someone else attend in your place or complete the task for you, you can delegate the message.

When you delegate an appointment or task, you pass it along to someone else without necessarily keeping a copy for yourself. To delegate an appointment or task, right-click the item and choose Delegate from the QuickMenu.

Here's how to delegate an appointment or task when the item is open:

1. Select Actions.

2. Select Delegate. A new message is created, identical to the message you received, except that the word *Delegated* is appended to the subject line.

3. Address the message to the person to whom it is being delegated.

4. Click Send. You will be asked if you want to keep a copy of the item in your Mailbox.

5. Answer Yes or No.

The person who sent you the message can find out that you have delegated the item by checking the message status. The "Delegated" status will appear along with the name of the person to whom you delegated the appointment or task.

Creating Recurring Items Using Auto-Date

The GroupWise Auto-Date (Recurring) feature enables you to send recurring appointments, tasks, or note messages. Auto-Date enables you to send one message that applies to many different days. For example, you can use an appointment Auto-Date to schedule a staff meeting that occurs every Wednesday at 9:00 a.m., or you can use a task Auto-Date to make sure staff members turn in a report on a certain day each month. You can also send a note configured with Auto-Dates to remind employees which day is payday.

There are three different ways to create Auto-Date messages:

▶ By dates

▶ By example

▶ By formula

For the most part, the by-example method makes the by-formula method obsolete. Therefore, we do not discuss the by-formula option.

By Dates

The by-dates Auto-Date method is the easiest to use and understand. When you choose this method, a calendar opens up for the current year, and you click the dates on which you want the appointment, task, or note to appear. You can click the Year button to advance the calendar to the next year.

To create an Auto-Date Calendar entry using the by-dates method, follow these steps:

1. Open a new appointment, task, or note message.

2. Fill in the To, Subject, and Message fields.

3. Click the Actions pull-down menu.

4. Select Auto-Date. The Auto-Date dialog box appears, as shown in Figure 7.7. (The Dates tab is active by default.)

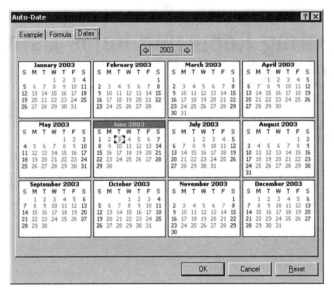

FIGURE 7.7
You can use the Date tab of the Auto-date feature to set up recurring appointments, notes or tasks.

5. Click all dates when the appointment, task, or note should appear.

6. Click OK.

7. Click Send to send the message.

The by-dates method of setting recurring Calendar items is the most flexible and easy to use of the three methods.

By Example

Use the by-example Auto-Date method when you want to send appointments, tasks, or notes for dates that follow a regular pattern. For instance, a by-example Auto-Date could be used to schedule a meeting that occurs on the third Tuesday of every month.

The by-example Auto-Date requires some experimenting to get the hang of it. The following example should help you get a sense of how it works.

One of the most common ways people use Auto-Date is to create personal notes reminding themselves when it's payday. The following steps show how to use Auto-Date to create a personal note for a payday that occurs on the 1st and 15th day of every month, unless the payday falls on a weekend. If the 1st or 15th falls on a weekend, the payday occurs on the preceding Friday. Here is what you would do:

1. Click Window.

2. Click Calendar view to see your personal calendar.

3. Double-click in the Reminder Notes field to open a new posted reminder note message.

4. Click Actions.

5. Click Auto-Date.

6. Choose the Example tab.

7. In the Start field, enter the date when the Auto-Date period should begin.

8. In the End field, enter the date when the Auto-Date period should end.

9. Click all months in the Months field to indicate that the paydays occur every month.

10. Click the drop-down list box named Days of the Week and select instead the Days of the Month setting. The dialog box changes, enabling you to specify certain days in the month for the note.

11. Highlight Monday, Tuesday, Wednesday, Thursday, and Friday to indicate that the note should only appear on a weekday.

12. Choose On/Before from the drop-down list located below the days you have highlighted. The On/Before option tells GroupWise that the note can only appear on or before the day you specify. For example, if the 15th falls on a Saturday, the note should appear on the previous Friday.

13. Click 1 and 15 in the calendar to indicate the dates when the note should appear. Figure 7.8 shows how the Auto-Date dialog box should look at this point.

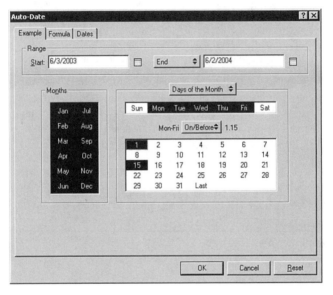

FIGURE 7.8
The Payday note will create a note in recipients' calendars for the whole year.

14. Click OK.

15. Fill in the remaining message fields in the reminder note and click Send.

A note will appear in your Calendar on each day that meets the Auto-Date criteria during the period you specified in the date range fields.

When you send an appointment message or note created using Auto-Date, one message is created and sent by the GroupWise system for every date that meets the Auto-Date criteria. If you send an Auto-Date appointment message that occurs every Friday during a year interval, 52 separate appointments will appear in each recipient's Mailbox. The recipient will be given the option to accept all instances at once or to accept or decline each message individually.

The Online Help system includes a guide for using the Auto-Date feature. To access the guide, follow these steps:

1. Click Help.
2. Click User's Guides.
3. Choose the GroupWise Basics option.
4. Select the "Schedule a Recurring Event" guide.

The by-example method lets you create regularly recurring Calendar items.

Multi-User Calendars

GroupWise provides for an office administrator to manage Calendars for several other GroupWise users. Before you can manage another GroupWise user's Calendar, the other user must give you proxy access to his or her GroupWise Calendar. The instructions for granting proxy access are provided in the next chapter.

To manage multiple users' Calendars, you use the Multi-User button on the Toolbar that displays when you open your Calendar folder, as illustrated in Figure 7.9.

Here's how to add users to the Multi-User Calendar display:

1. Verify that the users you want to add have granted you proxy access to their Calendars.
2. Click the Add User button. The Multi-User List dialog box displays (see Figure 7.10).
3. Enter the users' names in the Name field, or use the Address Book to select the users.
4. Click the up- and down-arrow buttons to change the order in which the users display in the Calendar.
5. Click OK. You'll see multiple users' Calendars displayed, as shown in Figure 7.11.

CHAPTER 7   Group Calendaring and Task Management

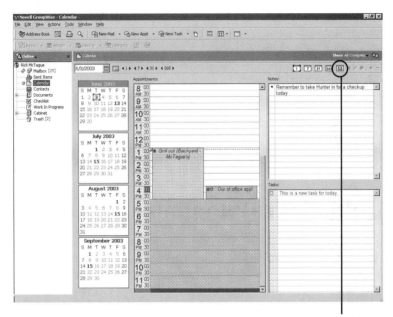

Multi-User button

FIGURE 7.9
The Multi-User button allows you to see other's Calendar information.

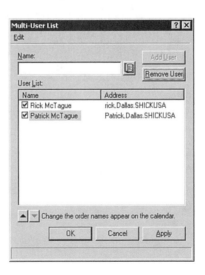

FIGURE 7.10
You can select the users to display in the Multi-User Calendar view with
this dialog box.

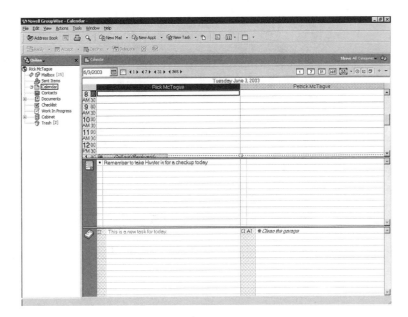

FIGURE 7.11
You can view other user's Calendar information using Multi-User.

TIP You can alter the Multi-User Calendar display by clicking the message type buttons that appear on the Calendar's Toolbar. You can choose to display any combination of multiple users' appointments, reminder notes, and tasks. You can also choose the order in which the tabs appear in your Calendar view by right-clicking the Toolbar and choosing Properties.

Printing Calendars

GroupWise provides powerful Calendar printing capabilities. You can choose from several popular formats, including formats familiar to users of the Franklin Quest day planners.

Here's how to print your GroupWise calendar:

1. Open the Calendar folder in the main GroupWise screen.
2. Click File.
3. Click Print Calendar. The Print Calendar dialog box, shown in Figure 7.12, displays.

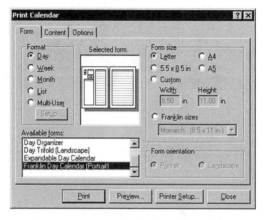

FIGURE 7.12
You can print out your Calendar items using this dialog box.

4. In the Format field, select from Day, Week, Month, List, or Multi-User.

5. In the Available forms field, select your desired form.

6. Select a form size and a form orientation.

7. Click the Content tab.

8. Select the starting date, the number of weeks (if the Week format is selected), the content, and the display option.

NOTE The preceding step depends on the Print format you have selected. If you are printing the Day calendar, it will display as the number of days; if months, the number of months.

9. Click the Options tab.

10. Specify the custom options. Among the options you can select are headers, footers, and page numbers.

11. Click Print when you're done.

Figure 7.13 shows the preview screen for the popular Franklin Quest Day Calendar printing format.

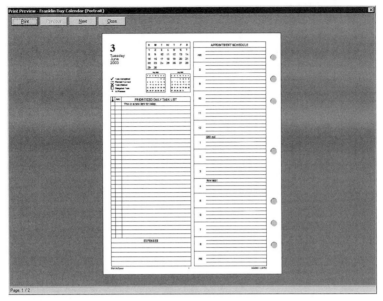

FIGURE 7.13
The Franklin form can be used to print your Calendar information.

The print options for the GroupWise Calendar provide several different styles, options, and content configurations. You should try several to see which works best for you.

Summary

In this chapter we discussed the appointments, notes, and tasks that make up the group calendaring features of GroupWise. We also discussed Busy Search, tracking items you send to others, and printing Calendar items. In Chapter 8 we will get into the advanced features of GroupWise 6.5 that will make you a true power user.

Advanced Features

This chapter introduces you to the advanced features of GroupWise, including Cache Mode, rules, Proxy, send options, My Subject, discussions, message threading, appearance options, Notify, Internet features, security, Junk Mail Handling, Mailbox size management, and Mailbox repairing.

We call this our "kitchen sink" chapter because of the variety of topics covered here. Once you master the concepts of this chapter, however, you will likely become known as the GroupWise Guru among your co-workers.

We have divided this chapter into two halves. The first deals with the features for using GroupWise day to day that will make you more productive, such as rules and Proxy. The second covers advanced Mailbox configuration and maintenance features, such as Internet accounts and repairing your Mailbox.

Advanced Features: User Productivity

In the first half of the chapter, we will cover those advanced features that add to your productivity. We will cover the following advanced features in this section:

▶ Rules (automatic actions on messages)

▶ Proxy (allowing access to your Mailbox or accessing someone else's Mailbox)

▶ Send Options (such as status tracking or notification)

▶ Advanced Security (using encryption)

▶ My Subject (customizing a received message)

▶ Discussions (threaded posted messages around one topic)

▶ Notify (alerts on received messages)

GroupWise Rules

GroupWise is capable of managing most of your messages for you (even while you are not logged in to the system) through GroupWise rules. Rules enable you to move messages to folders, generate automatic replies, forward messages, and delete messages. You can also set up rules to manage your Calendar items automatically. For example, you can create a rule that accepts all the tasks your boss sends you (always a good idea) or a rule that automatically declines appointments scheduled after 5:00 p.m. (an even better idea).

This chapter won't list all the possible rules you can create, but it will explain the basics for setting up rules and show you a few useful examples.

To create a rule, follow these steps:

1. Select Tools, Rules, New. The New Rule dialog box shown in Figure 8.1 appears.

2. Fill in the fields and choose Save.

The rule is added to your *Rules List* and is automatically activated. (The black check mark in the box next to a rule indicates that the rule is activated, as shown in Figure 8.2.)

You can use the Rules dialog box to change a rule in the following ways:

▶ To modify a rule, select the rule and then click the Edit button. You can then change any of the parameters of the rule. Choose Save to complete your changes to the rule.

FIGURE 8.1
The sample rule created moves all high-priority messages to a folder named Do it Now.

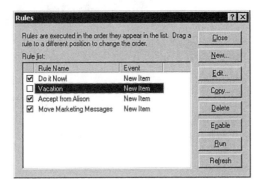

FIGURE 8.2
Your Rules List shows all the rules you have saved, both active and inactive.

▶ To copy or delete a rule, select the rule and then click the Copy button or the Delete button. You can use the Copy feature to create additional rules, based on the original rule. For example, if you create a rule that routes all messages from a specific user to a specific folder, you could copy this rule for messages from another user that you want routed to a different folder (without having to create a new rule from scratch).

▶ To activate or deactivate a rule, click the check box next to the rule or use the Enable/Disable button to the right of the Rules List.

▶ To run a rule, select the rule in the list and then click the Run button. You need to use the Run button only when you create a new rule that acts on messages already in your Mailbox.

TIP Your rules are executed in the order in which they appear in the Rules List (see Figure 8.2). This is important when, for example, you have a "delete" rule before a "reply" rule. To change the order in which the rules are executed, click a rule in the Rules dialog box and drag it to a new position.

Figures 8.3, 8.4, and 8.5 show examples of commonly used rules.

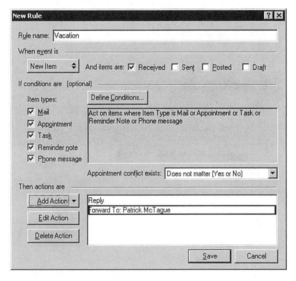

FIGURE 8.3
A commonly used *vacation* rule that will automatically reply to the sender and forward the message to someone.

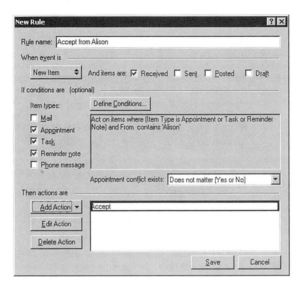

FIGURE 8.4
A rule that automatically accepts appointments from a specified person.

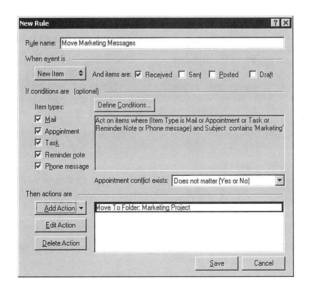

FIGURE 8.5
Another commonly used rule that automatically moves messages to a folder based on the subject of the message.

Table 8.1 describes the available actions that you can assign to a rule, under the Add Action button. It also describes the information needed to completely specify the action.

TABLE 8.1   Actions Assignable to a Rule

ACTION	DESCRIPTION	INFORMATION NEEDED
Send Mail	Generates a new mail message	Complete the Mail Message dialog box (recipient, subject, message, and so on)
Forward	Forwards a copy of the message	Identify the recipient of the forwarded message, along with a comment
Delegate	Delegates the appointment, reminder, note, or task to another individual	Complete the Delegate dialog box with a comment to both the sender of the original message and the person to whom you are delegating this item
Reply	Generates a reply to the sender	Specify the recipient (sender or all recipients), indicate whether to include the original message, and enter a reply message (subject and message body)
Accept	Accepts the appointment, reminder, or note	Select whether to show the accepted item as Free, Busy, Tentative, or Out of the Office, and enter a comment to the sender
Delete/Decline	Deletes the message or declines the Calendar event	Enter a comment for the sender's Sent Items folder
Empty Item	Purges the item from the Trash folder	N/A
Move to Folder	Moves the message to a folder	Select the folder and click Move
Link to Folder	Places a copy of the message in a folder	Select the folder and click Link
Mark as "Private"	Places a "Private" lock on the item	N/A

TABLE 8.1 Continued

ACTION	DESCRIPTION	INFORMATION NEEDED
Mark as "Read"	Changes the status of the item to "Opened"	N/A
Mark as "Unread"	Changes the status to "Unopened"	N/A
Stop Rule Processing	Ends the processing of a rule	N/A

The Rule feature is highly customizable and allows you a significant amount of automation for your Mailbox.

TIP For more information on how other users have employed GroupWise rules, see the GroupWise Cool Solutions Community at www.novell.com/coolsolutions/ gwmag/ or click the "Cool Solutions Web Community" item on the Help menu.

Using the Proxy Feature

The Proxy feature lets you access other users' GroupWise messages and Calendars. With this feature you can also permit others to view your GroupWise messages.

Remember, your Mailbox contains all your GroupWise information: email messages, Calendar items, sent items, deleted messages, personal folders, rules, and so forth.

There are two general steps to setting up the Proxy feature:

1. Specify access to a Mailbox. Who can access what information, and how it can be accessed. (Read, Write, or both?)

2. Start a Proxy session. The process of opening up someone else's Mailbox.

You cannot access others' Mailboxes until they have given you access privileges to their Mailboxes. Likewise, others cannot access your Mailbox until you have granted them access privileges.

NOTE Be sure you completely understand the available access privileges before granting them to others. If you are too liberal when granting rights to your Mailbox, other users can send messages that appear to be from you and they could possibly modify your setup and grant other individuals Proxy rights—and that could be bad.

Setting a Password

To provide the highest level of security for your Mailbox, we strongly recommend setting a password and thereafter keeping that password secure.

NOTE If you use Proxy to access someone else's Mailbox, the password is not required to gain access. The password feature protects against unwanted access by someone to whom you have not granted any access rights.

Setting a password is an option you establish through the Tools menu. (We discuss how to set other options and defaults in Chapter 11, "Customizing GroupWise.")

To set a password on your Mailbox, follow these steps:

1. Select Tools, Options and double-click the Security icon.

2. Enter a password in the New Password field and in the Confirm New Password field. Choose OK to set the password. The next time you start GroupWise, you will need to type in your password. If you select the No Password Required with eDirectory option, you will not be prompted to enter a password when you access your own Mailbox if you are logged in to eDirectory.

TIP Your password is case sensitive and is unknown to the administrator or anyone else. If you forget your password, the administrator can remove it or set a new one, but usually not until you've endured a lengthy lecture about computing practices and protocols.

Granting Access to Others

To grant other GroupWise users access rights to your Mailbox, follow these steps:

1. Select Tools, Options and double-click the Security icon.

2. Choose the Proxy Access tab.

3. Click the Address button next to the Name field to start the Address Selector. Double-click the user you want to grant access to. Choose OK to add the user to the access list (see Figure 8.6).

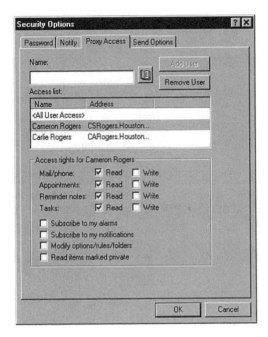

FIGURE 8.6
The Proxy feature lets you grant others access to your GroupWise Mailbox.

NOTE The All User Access entry in the Access List box lets you grant blanket rights to all other GroupWise users. Use extreme caution when selecting this option.

---

4. With the user in the Access List highlighted, select the appropriate access. (See Table 8.2 for a description of the access rights.) Click OK and then Close to apply the rights.

5. To remove a user from the Access List, highlight the user in the Access List and click the Remove User button.

6. To change someone's access, highlight the user in the Access List, change the rights, click OK, and then click Close to complete the change.

TABLE 8.2 Proxy Access Fields

ITEM TYPE	ACCESS RIGHT
Mail/Phone	Read: Read messages in your Mailbox folder. Write: Write email and phone messages in your stead.
Appointments	Read: Read posted and group appointments from your Calendar. Write: Create posted appointments and invite others to meetings in your stead.
Reminder Notes	Read: Read personal and accepted notes from your Calendar. Write: Create personal notes and send notes in your stead.
Tasks	Read: Read posted tasks and assigned tasks from your Calendar or To Do List. Write: Create posted tasks or send tasks to others in your stead.
Subscribe to My Alarms	Enable users to have alarms for your appointments.
Subscribe to My Notifications	Enable users to have notifications for all messages you receive displayed on their computers.
Modify Options/Rules/Folders	Enable users to change your preferences (password, rules/folders, Mailbox access, defaults, and so on), create rules for your Mailbox, and change your folder structure.
Read Items Marked Private	Enable users to read any item (mail message, marked "Private" appointment, task, or note) that is marked "Private."

NOTE You should only grant Modify Options/Rules/Folders rights to very trustworthy individuals. These rights enable users to change your password and grant others access to your Mailbox.

Starting a Proxy Session

With the Proxy feature, you can access a person's entire Mailbox and perform other activities within the parameters allowed by the permissions the other GroupWise user has granted to you. Having full access to someone else's Mailbox does not mean you can view only the person's messages and Calendar items. You can also send mail messages as that user, access the user's sent items, personal folders in the Cabinet, and deleted messages in the Trash, and edit the user's rules and preferences.

After you are through viewing someone else's Mailbox, you need to end the Proxy session to view your Mailbox again. Optionally, you can open an additional GroupWise window for the other user while keeping your Mailbox open. (This technique is explained in more detail in the next section.)

To start a Proxy session and view someone else's Mailbox, follow these steps:

1. Click File, Proxy or click the icon next to the online status indicator and select Proxy.

2. Type in the username of the user whose Mailbox you want to access. Alternatively, you can click the Address Book icon next to the Name field, double-click the user from the Address Selector, and choose OK.

The Proxy session starts. Note that the status changes to "Proxy" and the name of the user whose Mailbox you are accessing appears in the GroupWise title bar, as shown in Figure 8.7.

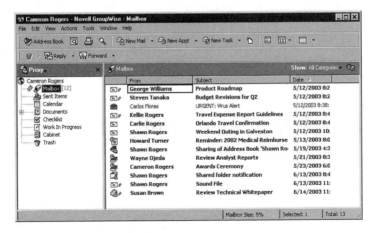

FIGURE 8.7
The GroupWise main screen indicates Proxy access.

To end the session and view your Mailbox again, click the Proxy icon and select your name. Your Mailbox will open.

Opening Multiple Windows

By default, your main GroupWise window will change to the Mailbox you are accessing with the Proxy feature. This default can be tedious if you need to view multiple Mailboxes. In this case it is useful to open a different GroupWise window for each active Proxy session. This multiple-window feature lets you view many different Mailboxes and Calendars (with the Multi-User Calendar view) from your workstation.

TIP There are other reasons to open multiple GroupWise windows. For example, you can have one window for viewing the new messages in your Mailbox, another one showing your open Calendar, and a third window for viewing documents in the document library.

To open an extra GroupWise window (with your Mailbox open), follow these steps:

1. Select Window, New Main Window. A new, complete GroupWise window appears on your screen.

2. Click the Proxy icon and start a Proxy session with another Mailbox. This new window displays the Mailbox you are accessing.

3. You can access any of the open windows by choosing that window from the Window menu. Each window is labeled with the name of the user whose Mailbox is open.

NOTE As discussed in Chapter 7, "Group Calendaring and Task Management," you can use the Multi-User tab in the Calendar folder view to see multiple users' Calendar information on one screen.

Specifying Send Options

When you create any type of message—from mail messages to tasks—you can specify a number of different send options (in other words, options that affect the way GroupWise sends the message). These options fall into three categories: General, Status Tracking, and Security.

To apply one of the send options to a message you are creating, follow these steps:

1. Choose the Send Options tab before you choose Send. The Send Options page displays, as shown in Figure 8.8.

2. The general send options are displayed by default. Choose the Status Tracking or Security button to display those advanced options.

3. Select the desired options and then click the Mail tab to return to the message.

This message will be sent with the options you selected.

General Send Options

General options, shown in Figure 8.8, let you configure your outgoing messages, such as requesting a reply to a message within 4 days.

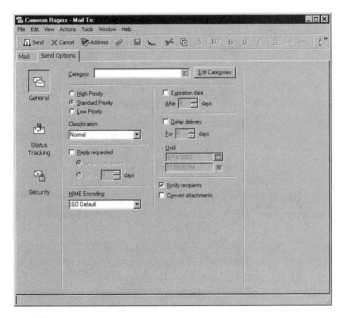

FIGURE 8.8
The General Send Options page lets you control your message delivery.

NOTE You can set any of these send options as the default. (Setting defaults is covered in Chapter 11.)

Table 8.3 lists the general send options. (Asterisks denote default options.) These options enable you to configure your outgoing messages.

TABLE 8.3 General Send Options

OPTION	AVAILABLE CHOICES	DESCRIPTION
Category	Dependent on configured categories	Lets you select a preestablished category for the message
Priority	High	Delivered before other messages
	*Standard	Normal delivery
	Low	Deliver after standard priority messages
Classification	*Normal	No security message
	Proprietary	"Security: Proprietary" placed at the top of the message
	Confidential	"Security: Confidential" placed at the top of the message
	Secret	"Security: Secret" placed at the top of the message
	Top Secret	"Security: Top Secret" placed at the top of the message
	For Your Eyes Only	"Security: For Your Eyes Only" placed at the top of the message
Reply Requested	*Not Selected	No reply requested
	When Convenient	Reply requested when convenient
	Within n days	Reply requested within n days (up to 99)
MIME Encoding	*ISO Encodes	Converts attachments using ISO MIME
	UTF8	Use Unicode Transformation Format to encode/convert attachments
	(Other options are available depending on system configuration.)	
Expiration	*Not Selected	Message deleted from Mailbox by the recipient
	After n days	Message deleted from Mailbox after n days (up to 999)

TABLE 8.3   Continued

OPTION	AVAILABLE CHOICES	DESCRIPTION
Delay Delivery	Delay n days Until date/time	Deliver after n days Delay message delivery until specified date and time
Notify Recipients	On/Off	Use the Notify program to tell recipients that this message has been delivered
Convert Attachments	On/Off	Convert file attachments that pass through a gateway

Status Tracking Options

The Status Tracking options, shown in Figure 8.9, let you select the amount of information you want made available to you as the sender of a message, such as tracking all information versus just the delivery date and time of the message.

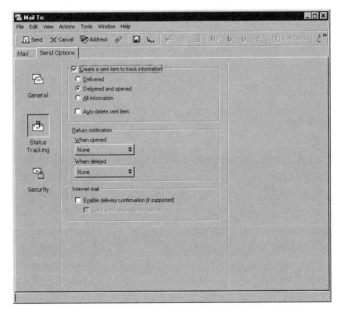

FIGURE 8.9
The Status Tracking page lets you control your message delivery.

CHAPTER 8   Advanced Features

Table 8.4 summarizes the Status Tracking options. (Asterisks denote default options.)

TABLE 8.4   Status Tracking Options

OPTION	AVAILABLE CHOICES	DESCRIPTION
Create a Sent Item to Track Information	*On/Off	Create an item in your Sent Items folder (or not)
Delivered	On/Off	Status for Delivered date and time
*Delivered and Opened	*On/Off	Status for Delivered and Opened
All Information	On/Off	Delivered, Opened, Deleted, Accepted, Declined, Completed, Downloaded, Transferred, Retracted, Replied, and Emptied
Auto Delete Sent Item	On/*Off	Delete the message from the sender's Sent Items folder after all recipients have deleted it from their Mailboxes
Return Notification When Opened, When Accepted, When Declined, When Completed, or When Deleted (The options differ depending on item type.)	*None	No notification or mail
	Mail Receipt Notify Notify and Mail	New message in Mailbox Notification Notification and new message in Mailbox
Internet Mail	Enable Delivery Confirmation (If Supported)	Lets you receive a delivery confirmation in your Message Information screen for messages sent through the Internet when the receiving system supports delivery confirmation

TABLE 8.4   Continued

OPTION	AVAILABLE CHOICES	DESCRIPTION
	Send Notifications to My Mailbox	Lets you receive a delivery confirmation mail message if confirmation is supported

Security Options

The Security page relates to the security aspects of the messages you send, as shown in Figure 8.10.

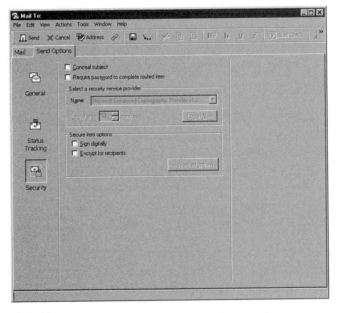

FIGURE 8.10
The Security page lets you add security to your message.

The Conceal subject security option hides the message subject when viewing the Mailbox. The subject is only visible when the recipient opens the message.

The Require password to complete routed item option causes each recipient of a routed item to enter his or her GroupWise password after marking a routed item "Completed." The message is not forwarded to the next recipient unless the password is entered correctly.

The Select a security service provider option is only available if you have installed a supported security provider. If this option is not available, you have either not installed a security provider or your security provider does not support the options.

GroupWise works with security software available from third-party companies. The following security products are supported:

► Entrust 4.0 or higher from Entrust Technologies Inc.

► Microsoft Base Cryptographic Provider version 1.0 or higher. To use this provider, you must also obtain a security certificate from an independent Certificate Authority.

► Microsoft Enhanced Cryptographic Provider version 1.0 or higher. To use this provider, you must also obtain a security certificate from an independent Certificate Authority.

Contact your administrator to determine whether you have these products available to your GroupWise system.

You can add security to the items you send by using digital signatures or encryption.

The Sign digitally option lets you add a digital signature to your email message. When you add a digital signature to your message, recipients of the message who have an S/MIME-enabled email system can verify that the item actually originated from you.

The Encrypt for recipients option lets you digitally encrypt the message. This assures you that only recipients who have an S/MIME-enabled email system will be able to read the contents of the message.

You use your security certificate (explained later) to digitally sign your messages. You use other users' public security certificates to verify digitally signed items that you receive from them.

Security Certificates

A security certificate is a file that uniquely identifies a specific individual or organization. You must obtain a security certificate before you can send security items.

If you are using a Microsoft security provider, you can use your Web browser to obtain a security certificate from an independent Certificate Authority. If you are using Entrust as your security provider, you must use an Entrust certificate. You manage your certificates by clicking Tools, Options, Certificates.

A more in-depth discussion of security certificates is found in Chapter 11. Refer to that chapter for the default security options you can set for your GroupWise client.

> **NOTE** Novell provides a list of Certificate Authorities you can use with GroupWise at www.novell.com/groupwise/certified.html.

Marking Items Private

Sometimes you want to store information in your Mailbox that is private and you don't want your closest Proxy associates to see it. You can add an extra measure of control on any item in your Mailbox—email messages, appointments, tasks, notes, or any other message—by marking the item "Private." Marking an item Private does not change the way GroupWise handles the message, but it does place a lock on the item.

You should mark items Private when you have granted others access to your Mailbox. Unless you grant them the right Read Items Marked Private, any item you mark as Private will be invisible to them. To mark an item Private when composing the message, click Actions, Mark Private, or you can simply press F8.

> **NOTE** If the item being marked Private is a Calendar item, a padlock icon appears next to the item. If it is any other kind of item, no indication is given that the item is private, except for a check mark next to the Mark Private option under the Actions menu.
>
> To remove the Private setting, highlight the item and choose the Mark Private option under the Actions menu. This action removes the check mark.

My Subject

If you have ever received an email with an inaccurate or unrelated subject to the message, you'll be glad to know that GroupWise 6.5 provides you with the ability to change a subject to something you specify.

When you open a newly received message, click the Personalize tab, enter a new subject line on the My Subject line, and click Close.

> **TIP** This is especially handy when you have a rule that executes based on the content in the subject line.

Creating Discussions (Posted Messages)

In GroupWise terminology, a *discussion* is an advanced message type that enables related messages to appear under one umbrella, called a *discussion area*. These messages are posted in the discussion area's shared folder. You can view the history of the discussion participants' thought processes and the flow of their posted messages in a discussion area by using the Discussion Thread option under the View menu.

NOTE The terms *discussion*, *discussion area*, and *posted message* are synonymous.

Discussion areas and posted messages are created, stored, and accessed through shared folders.

TIP It is a good idea to include the word *discussion* in the name of the shared folder that will hold discussions to differentiate it from other shared folders.

To create a new discussion, follow these steps:

1. Highlight a shared folder in the Folders Area.
2. Choose File, New. Select Discussion/Note from the list of message types. As a shortcut, you can click the down arrow next to the Create New Mail button on the Toolbar and choose Posted Message.
3. Enter a subject line and message body, attach any files you wish, and click Post to place the new discussion in the shared folder.

TIP The posted discussion and all replies will have a "thumbtack and piece of paper" symbol next to them. This is the icon for a discussion message.

To read and reply to a discussion message, follow these steps:

1. Highlight a shared folder in the Folders Area.
2. Choose View, Display Settings, Discussion Thread. The discussions in this folder will appear, along with the replies in a nested fashion, as shown in Figure 8.11.
3. Double-click the discussion or reply you wish to read.

4. To create a reply, click Reply. If you would like to post a reply in the discussion area, choose either the Reply to Selected Subject option or the Reply to Original Discussion Topic option in the Reply dialog box. Your reply will appear under the appropriate message. If you wish to reply to any part of a discussion and not include your reply in the shared folder, select Reply Privately (outside discussion). Then send your reply as a regular mail message to the sender only or to all participants in the discussion.

NOTE If someone is currently creating a reply to a discussion message, no one else can read the discussion message until the reply is complete.

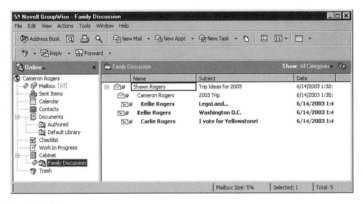

FIGURE 8.11
The Discussion view lets you see the history of a discussion in nested fashion.

Discussions are useful for quickly sharing information with a large group of people and for achieving smooth workflow. Discussions also provide a public, recorded history of communications at your organization.

Following Message Threads

When you have a shared folder full of discussions and replies, you need a quick-and-easy way to navigate through that information. The first task is to view the messages as discussions. This is done by clicking the shared folder that holds the discussions and choosing View, Display Settings, Discussion Threads.

To scan through the posted discussions and their replies easily, click the first message in the discussion (it will be left-justified on the screen and have a plus sign next to it). Then choose View, Threads. You will see a menu choice as displayed in Figure 8.12.

FIGURE 8.12
The Threads menu option allows you to navigate through discussions.

The Next option highlights the next item in the discussion, and Previous highlights the previous one. The Expand and Collapse options expand and collapse the listing of discussions and their replies, respectively.

Mailbox Setup and Maintenance Features

The features in this section have more to do with the configuration and maintenance of your Mailbox than they do with the message-by-message advanced features discussed in the first half of this chapter.

These features may require some assistance from your GroupWise administrator; feel free to investigate the powerful options available, such as Junk Mail Handling.

Here's a list of the features covered in this section:

- ▶ Internet-enabled features (accessing other email accounts, IMAP, and NNTP)

- ▶ Junk Mail Handling (automatically moving unwanted messages to a Junk Mail folder)

- ▶ Managing Mailbox size (keeping track of the size of your Mailbox)

- ▶ Repairing your Mailbox (maintaining and fixing problems with your Mailbox)

Internet-Enabled Features

The GroupWise 6.5 client software has the ability to access multiple email accounts in addition to the GroupWise Mailbox on a GroupWise post office. This relieves you from using multiple email programs to access these additional accounts. In addition, you can access NNTP newsgroups with GroupWise.

NOTE From a storage perspective, once you access an Internet email account using GroupWise, the messages are stored in your GroupWise Mailbox, having been "pulled" from the Internet mail server. The exception to this is an IMAP4 mailbox, in which case the messages are copied from the IMAP server to your GroupWise Mailbox.

Enabling access to an Internet mail account using GroupWise is easy, provided you have the required setup information.

NOTE When you set up an Internet mail account, you are provided with certain information, such as the mailbox type (POP3 or IMAP), server name, your login name for the server, your password on that server, and the email address for the account. You will need all this information to set up access to the account using GroupWise. You can obtain this information from your Internet service provider (ISP) where your Internet mail account is located.

To access Internet mail accounts using GroupWise, you must be in either Cache or Remote Mode. Chapter 10, "Remote Access," discusses how to set up GroupWise for these modes.

Setting Up Internet Mail Accounts

From the GroupWise client, your Internet mail account messages will be stored in a separate personal folder, which is created when you enable this feature.

NOTE To learn more about personal folders, take a look at Chapter 5, "Message Management."

Your system administrator needs to allow you to set up Internet mail account access. Once this is done, you can follow these steps to set up access:

1. From the GroupWise client, choose Accounts, Account Options.

NOTE If GroupWise is running in Online Mode, the Accounts menu will not be displayed.

---

2. From the Accounts dialog box, choose Add.

3. Enter your country, area code, and outside line access number, if needed. Click Close.

4. From the Create Account screen, shown in Figure 8.13, enter a name for the Internet mail account. Because this is just a "label" for what you want to call this service, you can enter anything you'd like.

5. Select the type of Internet mail account (POP3 or IMAP, as provided by your ISP) and click Next.

6. As shown in Figure 8.14, in the Create Internet Account screen enter the following fields as provided by your ISP and click Next:

   ▶ **Incoming mail server**—This is the POP3 or IMAP server where your mail is stored.

   ▶ **Login name**—The ID provided to you to access the incoming mail server.

   ▶ **Outgoing mail server**—Usually the same as the incoming mail server, this server sends your mail out to the Internet.

   ▶ **Email address**—This is the email address for this Internet mail account.

▶ **From name**—The name you would like displayed in the
From field in messages you reply to that you receive in this
Internet mail account.

FIGURE 8.13
You use this dialog box to specify the account name and account type.

7. In the next screen you configure the method you'll use to access
your Internet mail account, either connecting through the LAN or
using your modem. Choose the appropriate method and click
Next.

8. In the Create Internet Account screen, shown in Figure 8.15, you
select the folder (by clicking the box next to the desired folder) and
place it within your GroupWise folder structure to hold incoming
mail for this Internet mail account. (You can also create a new folder by clicking the Create new folder for account option at the top
of the dialog box and entering a folder name when you click
Finish.)

9. Click Finish to complete the Internet mail account setup. Both
your regular GroupWise account (if previously configured) and the
new Internet mail account you just set up will be listed in the
Accounts box, as shown in Figure 8.16.

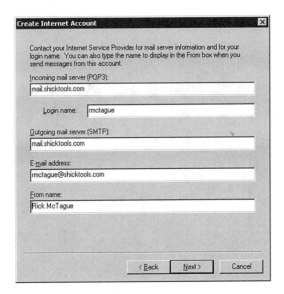

FIGURE 8.14
This dialog box is used to configure your Internet Mailbox connection information.

FIGURE 8.15
You can create a new folder to contain the Internet account messages.

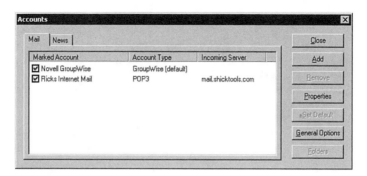

FIGURE 8.16
Your Internet account is now listed and ready to be accessed by
GroupWise.

Importing Messages, Addresses, and Account Settings

GroupWise 6.5 allows you to import items, addresses, and settings from
other email programs installed on your computer.

To import these items, open the GroupWise Importer by choosing Import
POP3/IMAP from the File menu. You'll see the screen shown in Figure
8.17. From there, follow these steps:

1. Select the email program to import from and click Next.

2. In the next screen, you select the email messages, account settings,
   or address book items to import, or you can choose a combination
   of these items. Click Next.

██ NOTE ██ The following steps assume all three options are selected (email messages,
account settings, and address book items).

---

3. In the next screen, you select the folders from the existing email
   program to import (see Figure 8.18). You can select all or some of
   the folders. Click Next.

4. In the following screen, you specify the name and location of the
   GroupWise folder that will hold your imported email messages (see
   Figure 8.19). In the Name field, enter a name for the folder and use
   the buttons on the right (Up, Down, Right, Left) to place the folder
   in your GroupWise Mailbox. Click Next.

FIGURE 8.17
This dialog box lets you choose which email program you want to import from.

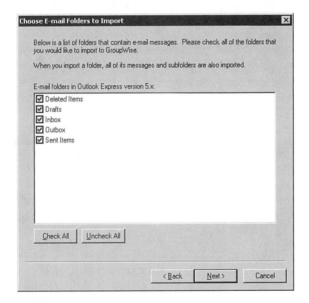

FIGURE 8.18
You can select the folders to import messages from.

FIGURE 8.19
This screen lets you configure the folder that the messages will be imported into.

5. In the next screen, you will name the new personal address book that will hold your imported addresses. Enter a name for the new address book and click Next.

6. Next, you will import the settings for the email program installed on your computer, which in this case is Outlook Express (see Figure 8.20). Click the check box next to the account name you wish to import settings from. You can also rename this account by clicking the Rename button, entering a new account name in the resultant dialog box, and clicking OK. Click Next.

7. In the Choose Folders for New Accounts screen, shown in Figure 8.21, you determine which GroupWise folder will hold the messages sent to that email account. It is a good practice to make a new folder for the account. Click the Change Folder button and then click the check box next to an existing folder (if desired) or click the Create New Folder for Account button to enter the name and location of a new folder. Click Next.

FIGURE 8.20
You can select the account to import settings from in this screen.

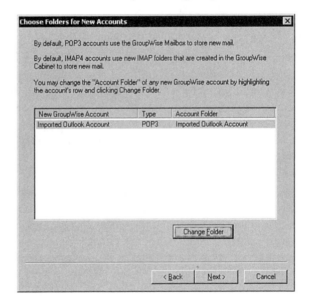

FIGURE 8.21
This screen lets you set up a new folder to hold the messages for the imported account.

8. You will then see a summary page, similar to the one shown in Figure 8.22, of all your selections. If you would like to make changes, use the Back button to do so. Once everything is satisfactory, click Next to begin the import. You will see a new screen with status bars for the import as it happens. The amount of time this will take depends on the number and size of the email messages and addresses you are importing.

FIGURE 8.22
You will see the summary page before beginning the import.

9. Once you have finished the import, you will see a results screen that displays the success or any errors of the import. Click Done to end the GroupWise Importer.

10. You will now have the following items (assuming you selected all three import sources):

   ▶ Email messages imported into a folder you specified.

   ▶ A new personal address book containing the addresses you imported.

> ▶ A new account for GroupWise to get messages from based on the settings you imported. Accessing and using the new account is identical to accessing and using an account you create manually. We cover that in the next section.

Congratulations! You have imported your other email program's settings into GroupWise, and you are now ready to use GroupWise to access the outside email account.

Accessing and Using Internet Mail Accounts

Using the Internet mail account with the GroupWise client is as easy as using any other personal folder. You can read, forward, reply to, delete, and otherwise manage your Internet mail just like you can any other GroupWise message.

To get your new email messages from your Internet mail account, from the Accounts menu, choose Send/Retrieve, All Marked Accounts or Send/Retrieve, <Internet Account Name>.

Your computer will use the connection method you set up earlier to establish a connection with the mail server, retrieve your new messages, and send outgoing messages.

IMAP Folders

IMAP (also known as *IMAP4*) is another type of Internet mail account that provides the use of folders and other advantages over traditional POP3 mailboxes. GroupWise can be used as an IMAP mail client, as described in "Setting Up Internet Mail Accounts" earlier in the chapter.

If you have an IMAP mail account, IMAP folders can be used to store and organize the IMAP messages. One benefit to IMAP mailboxes is the fact that messages are still available on the mail server after the IMAP mail client has retrieved them.

To set up an IMAP folder, follow these steps:

1. Determine where you would like to place the IMAP folder in your folder structure.

2. Highlight the "parent" folder under which you want to place your IMAP folder. Right-click and choose New Folder. Select IMAP Folder as the folder type and click Next.

3. From the Create Account screen, enter a name for the IMAP folder in the Account name field. One suggestion would be to use the name of your IMAP4 service provider. Click Next.

4. In the Create Internet Account screen, complete the following fields, as shown in Figure 8.23, and click Next:

> ▶ **Incoming mail server**—The name of the IMAP mail server, as provided to you by your ISP

> ▶ **Login name**—Your login name to the IMAP server

> ▶ **Outgoing mail server**—The name of the outgoing SMTP mail server, as provided to you by your ISP

> ▶ **Email address**—Your Internet mail address for this IMAP mail account

> ▶ **From name**—The name you wish to use to send all IMAP messages from

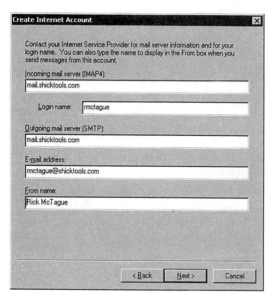

FIGURE 8.23
You use this dialog box to create an IMAP Internet account.

5. In the next screen, enter the connection method you wish to use to connect to the IMAP mail server and click Next.

6. In the Create Folder screen, you can enter a description and position the IMAP folder, as shown in Figure 8.24. When you are done, click Next.

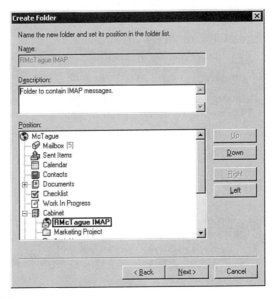

FIGURE 8.24
An IMAP folder can be placed where you decide in your Cabinet or folder structure, just like any other folder.

7. In the Display screen, you can configure the sort options, columns, and other customizable settings for this folder. These settings are described in Chapter 10. Click Finish after you have made your desired changes. Notice that the new IMAP folder has been created. To access your IMAP messages, simply click the IMAP folder. You will be prompted for your IMAP server login information, as shown in Figure 8.25.

8. Enter your login name (it will probably appear automatically) and your password. You can click the Save Password box, if desired. Click OK. Your IMAP messages will appear in the right pane of the GroupWise client.

FIGURE 8.25
You will need to log in to your IMAP service.

Usually, the default settings for the IMAP folder will suffice. To perform additional configuration of the IMAP folder, right-click the IMAP folder and choose Properties. The following tabs are used to configure the folder, as shown in Figure 8.26:

- ▶ **General**—Includes the email address, from name, and reply address

- ▶ **Server**—Includes the ISP IMAP server name, login information to the IMAP mail server, and the SMTP mail server name

- ▶ **Connection**—Specifies the method to connect to the IMAP mail server

- ▶ **Advanced**—Includes the root folder path (the folder on the IMAP server that contains your Mailbox folders), other folder options, IMAP and SMTP port information, and download options

- ▶ **Signature**—Includes signature information placed at the end of messages sent from your IMAP mail account

The IMAP mail protocol is a very popular mailbox standard, and GroupWise allows you to configure access to it as well as your corporate email.

NNTP Folders and Internet Newsgroups

Internet newsgroups (which use the NNTP protocol to send and receive news information) are a useful tool for sharing information related to a specified topic, such as car repair.

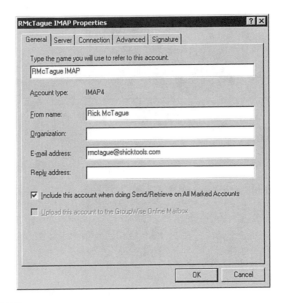

FIGURE 8.26
You can customize your IMAP folder using this dialog box.

GroupWise 6.5 can access NNTP newsgroup information and store the messages under a separate folder. The newsgroups are updated with new information as it becomes available. The newsgroups appear under the NNTP folder you create.

To set up an NNTP newsgroup folder, follow these steps:

1. Determine where in your folder structure you want the NNTP folder to be placed.

NOTE Separate "folders" under the main NNTP folder will be automatically created for the different newsgroups you subscribe to.

2. Right-click the "parent" folder under which you want to set up the NNTP folder and choose New Folder. Select NNTP Folder and choose Next.

3. In the Account Name field, enter a name for the NNTP folder, such as "Newsgroups," and choose Next.

4. In the Create News (NNTP) Account screen, shown in Figure 8.27, enter the following information and click Next:

▶ **News (NNTP) server**—This is the NNTP server name, as provided to you by your ISP.

▶ **My server requires authentication**—If your ISP's newsgroup server requires authentication, enter your ISP login name and password.

▶ **Email address**—This is your ISP email address.

▶ **From name**—This is the name your newsgroup postings will be from.

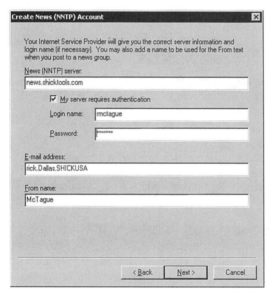

FIGURE 8.27
NNTP newsgroup account access is configured in this dialog box.

5. In the Create Internet Account screen, set up the method to connect to your ISP, just as you did for your Internet mail account, and click Next.

6. Enter a description and the position of the new NNTP folder and click Next. The name of the folder is the name you entered in the Account Name field in step 3 (see Figure 8.28).

7. Establish the folder's default settings, such as columns and the sort method, and click Finish. These settings are described in Chapter 11.

FIGURE 8.28
The NNTP newsgroup account is represented by an NNTP folder.

Now that you have set up the NNTP folder, you can begin to access newsgroups.

Accessing Newsgroups and Using the NNTP Folder
To subscribe to newsgroups, right-click the NNTP folder and choose Subscribe to Folders. Your computer will access your ISP's news server and pull down a listing of all available newsgroups, as shown in Figure 8.29.

NOTE Your computer may slow down and may even *appear* to stop responding while downloading the thousands of newsgroups (sometimes up to 50,000) on the news server. It should "come back to life" after a while, usually a few minutes. The count of newsgroups flashes at the bottom of the screen while downloading.

Select the newsgroup(s) you would like to subscribe to and click Subscribe. Use Ctrl+click to select multiple newsgroups. You can also search for newsgroups by entering search criteria in the Search for folders containing box and clicking the Search button.

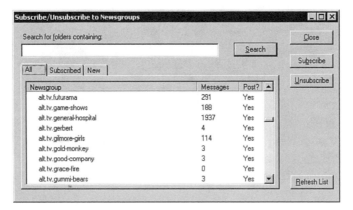

FIGURE 8.29
Your ISP's NNTP server will display the available newsgroups.

NOTE You can view the newsgroups you are subscribed to by clicking the Subscribed tab. To unsubscribe to a newsgroup, highlight it and click Unsubscribe.

Click close, and your newsgroup will appear as a subfolder under your NNTP folder.

Subscribing to Additional Newsgroups

To obtain a new list of available newsgroups, right-click the NNTP folder and choose Subscribe to Folders. Your computer will use the connection method you set up earlier to establish a connection with the newsgroup server and then update your NNTP folder with new newsgroups. You can then use the New tab to see any new newsgroups available. Use the steps described earlier to subscribe to a new newsgroup.

Accessing Newsgroup Messages

When you click the newsgroup, the messages it contains are listed in the right pane of the GroupWise window, as shown in Figure 8.30.

Newsgroup messages can be handled just like any other email. You can reply back to the sender, include the entire newsgroup as a recipient, or forward or delete the message, if desired. You can also create a new discussion topic in the newsgroup.

TIP You can copy (that is, *link*) a newsgroup message to another folder by clicking the message and dragging it to the other folder.

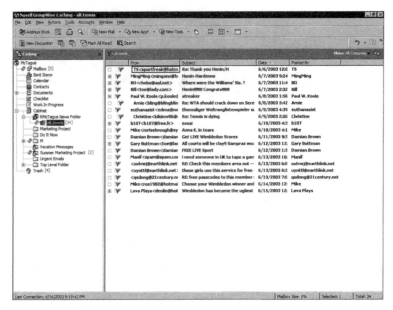

FIGURE 8.30
Newsgroup messages will appear within the subfolder under the main NNTP folder.

The actions you need to perform on the newsgroup itself are available to you by right-clicking the newsgroup:

▶ **Send/Retrieve**—This command updates your Mailbox with new messages, sending any replies or new discussions.

▶ **Reset**—This command is used to download entire newsgroups, with fresh copies of all postings.

▶ **New Discussion**—This command is used to enter a new discussion topic in the newsgroup.

▶ **Collapse All Threads**—This command collapses all messages; only the discussions will be listed.

▶ **Mark All Read**—This command is used to mark all postings as "Read."

▶ **Search on Server**—This command is used to search the news server for messages, by sender or subject.

These steps are adequate for accessing most newsgroups; additional configuration of the NNTP folder is covered next.

Additional Configuration of the NNTP Folder

Usually the default settings for the NNTP folder will suffice. To perform additional configuration of the NNTP folder, right-click the NNTP folder and choose Properties. The following tabs are used to configure the folder, as shown in Figure 8.31:

- ▶ **General**—Includes the email address, from name, reply address
- ▶ **Server**—Includes the ISP news server name and the login information to the news server
- ▶ **Connection**—Specifies the method to connect to the news server
- ▶ **Advanced**—Includes the NNTP port and download options
- ▶ **Signature**—Includes the signature information placed at the end of posted messages to newsgroups

FIGURE 8.31
Additional configuration of the NNTP folder is accomplished using this dialog box.

NNTP newsgroups are very good for accessing communities of information related to a specific interest or topic.

Junk Mail Handling

Email "spam" is one of the most annoying and time-consuming distractions of the digital age. It seems that once your email address gets into public circulation, there is no end to the useless and mailbox-clogging messages you receive.

New to GroupWise 6.5 is a feature known as *Junk Mail Handling* that lets you automate the process of dealing with spam, such as solicitations and other inappropriate messages.

NOTE Junk Mail Handling does not apply to internal email messages originating from users on your GroupWise system. It only applies to messages where the sender's email address is in the format of *name@domain*.com, *name@domain*.org, *name@domain*.net, and so on.

You can use the Junk Mail Handling feature in one of three ways:

▶ You can block individual email addresses or entire Internet domains. This is accomplished by adding these addresses or domains to a Block List. Messages received from these addresses or Internet domains are blocked and never arrive at your Mailbox.

▶ You can establish a Junk List and add individual email addresses or entire Internet domains to this list. Messages originating from these addresses or domains are delivered to the Junk Mail folder in your Mailbox. You can specify that items in this folder be automatically deleted after a certain number of days.

▶ You can route all messages from individuals who are not in your personal address books to the Junk Mail folder.

The Junk Mail folder is not enabled by default when you begin using GroupWise. It is created when you enable the Junk Mail Handling feature. If Junk Mail Handling options are enabled, this folder cannot be deleted.

Here's how to enable Junk Mail Handling and create the Junk Mail folder:

1. Click Tools, Junk Mail Handling.
2. In the Settings tab, enable the Junk Mail Handling features you want to implement.
3. Click the Junk List tab and add email addresses or Internet domains.

4. Click the Block List tab and add the email addresses or Internet domains you want to block.

5. Click OK.

To delete items from the Junk Mail folder, right-click the folder and select Empty Junk Mail Folder.

TIP When you receive an email message from a user or Internet domain that you want to add to either the Junk List or Block List, simply right-click the message, select Junk Mail, and then select either Trust Junk Sender or Block Sender.

A feature that works in tandem with Junk Mail Handling is the Trust List. You use the Trust List to perform the opposite task as the Block List. For example, suppose your main competitor is Superior Tools. Therefore, you decide to add the superiortools.com domain to your Block List so that you never receive messages from anyone employed at Superior Tools. However, you happen to have a good friend from high school who takes a job at Superior Tools. You can use the Trust List to allow email messages from your friend to bypass the block you placed on the superiortools.com domain.

Managing Your Mailbox Size

In most GroupWise environments, the system administrator will set size limits on the size of users' GroupWise Mailboxes. If you tend to keep every email you receive, if you simply don't keep up with the items coming into your Mailbox, or if you simply send and receive a lot of large file attachments, sooner or later you will run into the Mailbox size limit like a brick wall.

When this happens, you will need to archive or delete items from your Mailbox before you can send and receive GroupWise messages.

To find out your Mailbox size restriction and how much capacity you have remaining in your Mailbox, click Tools, Check Mailbox Size. The dialog box shown in Figure 8.32 will display.

NOTE The Check Mailbox Size option is not available in Online Mode, only in Caching and Remote Modes.

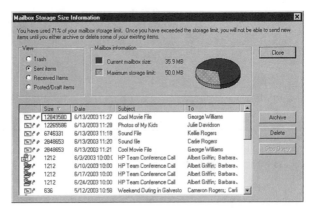

FIGURE 8.32
The Mailbox Storage Size Information dialog box lets you monitor the size of your Mailbox and quickly remove items that are taking up valuable space.

The Mailbox Storage Size Information dialog box is very useful. It allows you to quickly scan the locations where large messages are most likely to be found—the Sent Items and Received Items folders. It also sorts them by size in descending order.

Notice in Figure 8.32 that a few very large messages are clogging the Mailbox. If you click one of the large messages and select Delete, the message will be deleted from the source folder *and* emptied from the Trash (in other words, it's gone!).

Here are some additional tips for keeping your Mailbox size under control:

- ▶ Frequently empty your Trash.
- ▶ Frequently clean out your Sent Items folder.
- ▶ Sort your Mailbox items by size, and delete the largest items.
- ▶ Don't send messages with very large file attachments.
- ▶ Use the GroupWise Archive feature (explained in Chapter 5) to save messages to your hard drive or manually save attachments to your local hard drive and delete the message from your Mailbox.
- ▶ Monitor the Mailbox Size status bar located at the bottom-right area of the GroupWise main window. When it gets above 80%, start doing some housekeeping.

▶ If you send an email with a large attachment, be sure to delete that item from your Sent Items folder (not the recipient's Mailbox, of course) and then empty your Trash folder.

▶ Use the settings for automatically deleting and/or archiving your messages and Calendar information. These are described in Chapter 11.

You should make it a regular practice to clean out your sent items, your folders, and your Trash.

Repairing Your Mailbox

Although GroupWise is probably the most stable, fault-tolerant, and highly available messaging system on the market, the ability to create a copy of your Mailbox in either Cache or Remote Mode (Chapter 10) implies that occasional repairing of that local message store will need to take place.

NOTE If you only run GroupWise in Online Mode, your system administrator will take care of any repairs you might have to run on your Mailbox.

If you get a displayed notice stating "GroupWise has encountered a problem with your Mailbox and will repair it the next time you start GroupWise," you should shut down the GroupWise program and allow it to complete the automatic repair the next time you start it.

Most problems in GroupWise are transparent to you as a user. In other words, a small database problem can be detected and repaired by GroupWise before it ever manifests into something larger. However, larger problems may occasionally occur.

In addition, it is a good practice to run a periodic repair on your Mailbox even if no problems are occurring.

To perform the repair process, choose Repair Mailbox from the Tools menu. You may be prompted to perform a backup first (contact your system administrator to determine whether this needs to occur).

NOTE You must be in either Remote or Caching Mode and have the correct files available to see the Repair Mailbox menu option. Contact your administrator if you have questions on this.

You will then see the dialog box shown in Figure 8.33.

FIGURE 8.33
The Repair Mailbox options let you set up a maintenance process on your remote and/or caching Mailbox.

NOTE A detailed description of all the Repair Mailbox options is beyond the scope of this book. You should contact your GroupWise administrator for further information as to the many options.

For most repairs, you can select the defaults of Analyze/Fix Databases, with the Structure and Fix problems options selected. Also, keep the User and Message databases checked. Then click Run.

An amazing amount of technical information will be displayed; the repair (also known as *GroupWise Mailbox Maintenance*) may take a while to run, depending on the size of your Mailbox and the number of messages.

Once it is finished, you can peruse the log file as it is displayed and continue using GroupWise.

Summary

In this chapter, you saw how the powerful advanced features of GroupWise can help you be more productive using rules, Proxy, and sending options. We also covered how Internet accounts and newsgroups can be accessed using GroupWise, and how to monitor, manage, and repair your Mailbox. Chapter 9, "Document Management," will cover using GroupWise as a knowledge repository and document-management system.

CHAPTER 9

Document Management

Document management is very different from file management. In file management, you store your files in directories and subdirectories on your hard drive (or on a network drive). In document management, all documents are stored in a central location on a network. Instead of storing your documents in directories and subdirectories, you store them in a database system.

The document management capabilities built in to GroupWise make it a unique product in the email and groupware industry. The GroupWise document management service is a feature that lets you manage your documents in your GroupWise system. By integrating messaging and document management, GroupWise makes it easy to access documents and share them with others.

You can use GroupWise document management features to perform the following tasks:

- ▶ Store document files in the GroupWise system
- ▶ Access common files shared by members of your organization, company, or department and share your files with other users
- ▶ Maintain multiple versions of documents
- ▶ Search for documents stored in the system

NOTE GroupWise document management must be configured at the GroupWise system level before individual users can utilize the document management features. If you are unsure about whether document management is available at your organization, ask your system administrator. By default, document management is configured automatically in GroupWise 6.5.

Introducing Document Libraries

Document libraries are the heart of GroupWise document management systems. A library is a document storage location in a GroupWise system. The system administrator sets up each library. GroupWise users can store documents in libraries and can access shared documents placed there by other users.

A GroupWise library is similar to a real-world public library. If you need a particular book, you can quickly find out if it is at the library by checking the card catalog system. You can locate a particular book by its author, title, or subject matter. Instead of books, GroupWise libraries store documents. You can find a document in a GroupWise library by running a search based on its title, author, or subject, as well as a number of other criteria, collectively known as *document properties*.

Accessing Libraries

The system administrator sets up each library and determines library access privileges. For example, the administrator may set up a library that contains documents that everyone in the company needs to access, such as product marketing documents and expense report forms. The administrator might decide to grant only the View right so everyone can read the documents, but nobody except the administrator can change them. If your personal documents are stored in the library, the administrator needs to grant you different access rights for those documents. To manage your personal documents in a library, you need to be able to view, create, modify, and delete them.

If you have questions about what you can or cannot do within a library in your system, ask your administrator. By default, you should have access to at least one library with rights to store documents in that library.

Using Library Documents

After a document is placed into a library, it can only be accessed through GroupWise or through an application that uses GroupWise document management services (known as an *integrated application*). Integrated applications are automatically recognized by GroupWise when the GroupWise client is installed. You can determine which applications are integrated during the initial GroupWise setup. After GroupWise is installed, you can turn applications on and off for specific applications. (For a detailed explanation of working with integrated applications, refer to "About Integrating GroupWise with your Application" in the GroupWise Online Help system.)

Many Windows-based applications support GroupWise document management, such as the latest versions of Microsoft Word, Microsoft Excel, WordPerfect, and Quattro Pro.

If you need to work on a document when you are not logged into GroupWise, you must first "check out" the document from the library and place it in a directory or on a disk. When you are finished working on the document, you check it back into the library. We explain how to check documents in and out later in this chapter.

Documents stored in the library can be accessed in two ways: through document references in your GroupWise mailboxes or through document searches. A document reference is an item in your Mailbox with a document icon, similar to a mail message item with a mail icon. Both access methods are explained later in this chapter.

Setting a Default Library

A default library is the library where you store your documents by default. Although you might have access to many GroupWise libraries, you should specify one library as your default library. With GroupWise 6.5, you should already have a default library configured unless the standard configuration was modified by your administrator.

To set a default library, follow these steps:

1. Select Tools, Options.

2. Double-click the Documents icon. The dialog box shown in Figure 9.1 displays.

3. Highlight the library you want as your default library and click the Set Default button.

4. Click OK to save your settings and then click Close to exit Options.

FIGURE 9.1
Set your default library with the Documents Setup dialog box.

NOTE All libraries to which you have been granted the View right will appear in the list when you double-click the Documents icon. However, if you plan to store personal documents in your default library, you will need more than just the View right. Your system administrator can tell you which libraries are suitable for storing personal documents.

After you designate a default library, you can perform all the document management functions that are enabled by your rights assignments. Of course, before you can do anything with library documents, the documents must first be placed in the library. You place documents in a library either by importing them or by creating them in the library.

Importing Documents into a Library

Four methods exist for importing documents into a library: Quick Import, Custom Import, drag and drop, and the MAPI Send To feature.

NOTE Once a document is moved into a library, it can only be accessed through GroupWise or applications that integrate with GroupWise document management services. For example, if you create a document using Microsoft Word and save it in the library, you can still work on the document, but you must use the GroupWise document management dialog boxes to retrieve the document in Word. You can choose to copy documents into the library and maintain a copy outside of the library, but you must then decide how both versions will be kept current.

Using Quick Import

Quick Import copies your documents into the default library with the default document property settings. (Document properties are explained later in this chapter.) Quick Import does not let you customize documents individually. Use a Quick Import when you need to place many files into the library all at once and you are not concerned about customizing the document properties for each document.

Follow these steps to perform a Quick Import:

1. Select File, Import Documents. The dialog box shown in Figure 9.2 displays. Notice that the Quick Import option is selected by default.

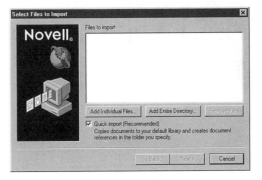

FIGURE 9.2
Place your documents in your default library using the Select Files to Import dialog box.

2. Click either the Add Individual Files button or the Add Entire Directory button.

3. If you selected the Add Individual Files option, navigate to the desired directory, highlight the files you want to import, and click OK. Repeat this step to add files from other directories.

4. If you selected the Add Entire Directory button, navigate to the desired directory or directories, and place check marks in the boxes next to the directories that contain files you want to import.

5. Repeat steps 2, 3, and 4 until all the files and directories are listed in the Select Files to Import dialog box.

6. Click Next when all files are listed in the Select Files to Import dialog box. The Create Document References dialog box appears, as shown in Figure 9.3.

7. Choose the Import without displaying documents in a folder option to import the documents into the library without creating document references in your Mailbox, or choose the Display documents in a folder option to create document references in a folder you specify.

8. If you chose to display the documents in a folder, click a check box in the Select folder for document references window to designate where the document references will appear. (Note: If you don't select a folder, a document reference will not be created.)

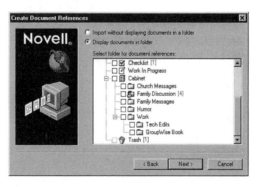

FIGURE 9.3
Specify where document references should reside with the Create Document References dialog box.

9. Click Next.

10. Click Finish to perform the import or click Back to modify your selected options. An import progress dialog box will display, showing you the status of the import and if any of the documents have failed to import correctly.

NOTE Quick Import places *copies* of documents into the library and leaves the source files in your directory structure unchanged.

Using Custom Import

Custom Import gives you much more control over importing documents into the library. Custom Import lets you perform the following actions:

- ▶ Specify which library you will import the documents into
- ▶ Specify document properties on a per-document basis
- ▶ Move or copy documents into the library

To import documents using Custom Import, follow these steps:

1. Select File, Import Documents.
2. Clear the Quick Import option by clearing the check box.
3. Click either the Add Individual Files button or the Add Entire Directory button.
4. If you selected the Add Individual Files option, navigate to the desired directory, highlight the files you want to import, and click OK. Repeat this step to add files from other directories. If you selected the Add Entire Directory button, navigate to the desired directory or directories and place check marks in the boxes next to the directories that contain files you want to import.
5. Repeat steps 2, 3, and 4 until all the files and directories are listed in the Select Files to Import dialog box.
6. Click Next when all files are listed in the Select Files to Import dialog box.
7. Click Next. The Import Method dialog box displays.
8. Choose between the Copy files into GroupWise and the Move files into GroupWise options and click Next.

NOTE The Move option removes the files from your directories and places them in the library. Be sure you don't accidentally move operating system or application files into the library.

9. (Optional) If you want a log file, select the Store All Status and Error Messages into a Log File option and specify a path and filename for the log file.

10. Click Next. The Select Library dialog box displays.

11. Select the library into which the files will be imported and click Next. The Create Document References dialog box displays.

12. Choose the Import without displaying documents in a folder option to import the documents into the library without creating document references in your Mailbox. Alternatively, choose the Display documents in a folder option to create document references in a folder you specify.

13. If you chose to display the documents in a folder, click a check box in the Select folder for document references window to designate where the document references appear. Click Next. The Set Document Property Options dialog box displays, as shown in Figure 9.4.

14. Choose the Prompt for properties of each document individually option if you want to set different document properties for each document you chose in steps 4 and 5. (This could be time consuming if you are importing many documents.) Alternatively, choose the Set properties using default values option to use the default properties for all documents.

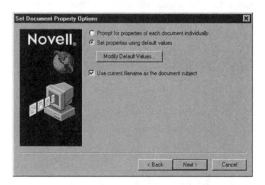

FIGURE 9.4
Specify customer parameters for your documents with the Set Document Property Options dialog box.

15. (Optional) Click the Modify Default Values button to establish default document properties for the files being imported.

16. If you don't want the document filename to be the document subject line for each document, clear the Use current filename as the

document subject check box. (If you clear the check box, you will be prompted to enter a subject for each document individually. Again, this could be tedious if you are importing several documents.)

17. Click Next. The Import Documents dialog box displays.

18. Click Finish to start the import process or click Back to modify your selections.

After the import finishes, document references will appear in the folder you selected (if you chose the Create Reference option) and your documents will be available from the library. Remember, others cannot access these documents because you have not set up sharing properties. Also, remember that you must be running GroupWise to access the documents in the library.

Using Drag and Drop

An alternative method for performing a quick import is to use the drag-and-drop technique to import your documents into a GroupWise library.

Here's how to use the drag-and-drop technique:

1. Open Windows Explorer.

2. Navigate to the file or files you want to import and then highlight the files using Shift+click or Ctrl+click.

3. Drag the files into a folder displayed in the GroupWise client.

These documents will be stored in your default library and document references will be created in the destination folder.

Using MAPI

You can use the MAPI Send To feature of Windows Explorer to import documents into a GroupWise library.

To use the Send To feature, follow these steps:

1. Open Windows Explorer.

2. Navigate to the file or files you want to import and highlight the files using Shift+click or Ctrl+click.

3. Click File, Send To, GroupWise Library.

The documents will be stored in your default library; however, document references will not be created.

Creating New Documents

In addition to importing existing documents into a GroupWise library, you can create new documents in a library.

To create a new document, follow these steps:

1. From the main GroupWise screen, select File, New.

2. Click Document. The New Document dialog box displays, as shown in Figure 9.5. When you create a new document, GroupWise prompts you to select a method for creating the document. You can select an application, a template, or a file. These options are explained in Table 9.1.

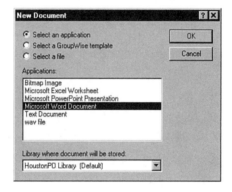

FIGURE 9.5
Create new documents in your default library with the New Document dialog box.

3. If you want to use a specific application to create the document, select the application and click OK. If you want to base the document on a template, select the template and click OK. If, instead, you want to base the document on a file, select the file and click OK. The New Document dialog box displays, prompting you to enter a subject for the document.

4. Enter a subject.

5. If you want to open the document, verify that the Open document now check box is selected and then click OK. GroupWise will open the application associated with the document type, the application, or the file extension, depending on the creation method you selected. For example, if the file extension is .doc, GroupWise will launch Microsoft Word.

TIP If you are opening an application that does not support GroupWise document management, you will get a warning stating that you are opening a nonintegrated application. Click OK to bypass the warning. If you don't want to see the warning again, click the Do not show this message again check box. You can use nonintegrated applications with GroupWise document management; just don't change the filename assigned by GroupWise when the document is open.

---

6. Create the document using the application.

7. Save the document using the assigned filename.

8. Close the application.

The document will be saved in the GroupWise library.

TABLE 9.1 Options for Creating a New Document

OPTION	FUNCTION
Select an Application	You can select an application to create a document based on that application. The Applications list box shows all the applications that are registered in the Windows Registry.
Select a GroupWise Template	A template is a file you use to create other documents, such as a word processing document preformatted with the company letterhead, or a spreadsheet file that is set up to calculate an expense report. You can select GroupWise templates to use a document in the library as the foundation of a new document. If you have documents that you often use as a basis for creating new documents, you can add them to the library and assign them the template document type. These templates will then appear in the templates list.

TABLE 9.1 Continued

OPTION	FUNCTION
Select a File	You can select a file anywhere on your system and use it as a foundation for a new document.

Creating Document References

When you create or import a document into the library, you have the option to create a document reference within a GroupWise folder. A document reference is similar to the icons you see in the Mailbox when you receive a mail message. It is a pointer you use to access the document in the library.

TIP If a document already exists in the library and you just want to create a document reference for it in your Mailbox, click File, New, Document Reference. You can also create a document reference by using the GroupWise Find feature to locate a document and drag the document to your Mailbox or other folder.

A document reference can exist in the same folder as GroupWise mail messages, or you can create folders in your Mailbox for your documents (just like you would create directories in a file system). By default, document references are placed in the Documents system folder.

Checking Out Documents

When you open a document from the library, the document is marked as In Use and cannot be opened and modified by other users. However, there may be times when you want to work on the document while you are not running GroupWise. For example, you may need to modify the document while at home or while on a business trip. In this situation, you would need to "check out" the document.

When you check out a document, the document is marked as In Use until you check it back in. The document cannot be modified by other users; the document, however, can be viewed by GroupWise users who have View rights.

You have two options when checking out documents:

- ▶ Check Out Only
- ▶ Check Out and Copy

If you choose the Check Out Only option, the document is marked as Checked Out in the library and cannot be modified by others, but it is not copied to a directory for you to access it.

If you choose the Check Out and Copy option, the document is copied to the directory you specify.

TIP To find out who has a document checked out of the library, right-click the document reference and choose Properties and then select the Activity Log tab.

Here are the steps to follow to check out a document:

1. Highlight the document reference in your Mailbox.

2. Click Actions, Check-Out. The dialog box shown in Figure 9.6 displays.

3. Type a filename for the document in the Checked out filename field. (By default, GroupWise uses the document number as the checked-out filename. You can specify a different filename.)

4. Enter a path for the document in the Checked out location field.

5. Click the Check Out button.

6. Click the Close button.

After you have checked out a document, you can open it from the directory and change it while you are not running GroupWise. The changes you make do not appear in the document in the library until you check it back in or update it.

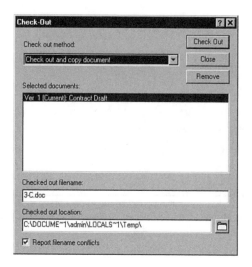

FIGURE 9.6
Use the Check-Out dialog box to copy a document to a local location for offline access.

Checking In Documents

After you have finished modifying a document that you have checked out from a library, you must check the document back in so that your changes are reflected in the library. Checking in a document also unlocks the document so other users can modify it.

TIP You can check in multiple documents at once by holding Ctrl and clicking multiple documents in the Documents to Be Checked In dialog box.

Here's how to check in a document:

1. Highlight the document reference in your Mailbox.

2. Click Actions and then Check-In. The dialog box shown in Figure 9.7 displays.

3. Choose the check-in method.

You have four options for checking in documents, as shown in Table 9.2. When you check in a document, you also have three options that relate to document versions, as shown in Table 9.3.

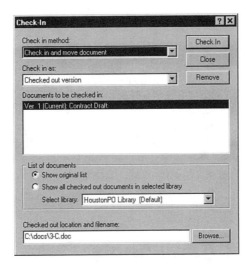

FIGURE 9.7
Use the Check-In dialog box to place an updated document back into the library.

TABLE 9.2 Check-in Method Options

OPTION	EXPLANATION
Check In and Move	Moves the document to the library and deletes it from the check-out location
Check In and Copy	Copies the document to the library and leaves a copy in the check-out location
Check In Only	Checks the document back in to the library but does not update the document in the library with any changes you made to the checked-out version
Update Without Checking In	Updates the document in the library with the changes you have made but does not unlock the document

TABLE 9.3 Check-in Version Options

OPTION	EXPLANATION
Checked-out Version	Keeps the same document version as the version you checked out
New Version	Lets you to specify a new document version

TABLE 9.3 Continued

OPTION	EXPLANATION
New Document	Lets you to create an entirely new document in the library and specify new document properties

Remember that if you are updating documents and you are connected to the GroupWise system, you do not have to go through the check-out, check-in process. When you open a document in the library, it is marked as In Use until you close the document. Other users cannot open and modify the document while you have it open. You only need to check out a document when you will be working on it while not connected to GroupWise.

Copying Documents

Use the document copy feature to create a document identical to one in the library and make changes without altering the original.

When you copy a document, you need to specify the new document's properties. You can manually specify the properties, or you can use the properties of the source document.

To copy a document, follow these steps:

1. Highlight one or more document references in your Mailbox.

2. Select Actions, Copy Document. The Copy Document dialog box displays, as shown in Figure 9.8.

3. Choose the library where the document will be copied to from the drop-down list.

4. Specify the method for creating the properties for the new document(s).

5. Click OK.

New document references appear in your Mailbox.

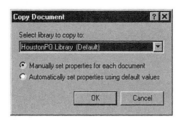

FIGURE 9.8
Use the Copy Document dialog box to make a duplicate of an existing document in a library.

Deleting Documents

If you have Delete rights, you can delete documents from the library.

You have three choices when deleting documents:

▶ **Remove document from folder**—This option deletes the document reference from your Mailbox, but the actual document remains in the library.

▶ **Delete the selected version from library**—This option deletes the document reference and the selected version of the document, but previous versions remain in the library.

▶ **Delete all versions of the document from library**—The document reference is removed from your Mailbox and all versions of the document are removed from the library.

GroupWise automatically deletes documents that have exceeded their defined document life, as specified in the document type definition. Each document type has an expiration date and expiration action (delete or archive). Your system administrator configures the expiration date and expiration action. As a GroupWise user, your only control over how long a document is stored is in selecting a specific document type. If you have questions about how long specific document types are stored, contact your GroupWise administrator.

To delete a document, follow these steps:

1. Highlight the document reference in your Mailbox.

2. Select Edit, Delete.

3. Choose the deletion method you want, as described earlier in the section.

4. Click OK.

The document is deleted according to the method you selected. If you get an error message that indicates the deletion failed, you do not have Delete rights to the document or library.

Searching for Documents

One advantage of document management is that it makes finding documents easy. Instead of hunting through directories and trying to recognize cryptic eight-character filenames, with GroupWise document management, you can search for documents using a number of different criteria, including a simple full-text search for specific words contained in the document.

Understanding Document Properties

Each document in a GroupWise library has a set of attributes that uniquely identifies the document, such as the author's name, the date the document was created, and the document type. These attributes are *document properties*. You use document properties to find documents that have been placed in a library.

You can set document properties when you import a document into the library or when you create the document. You can also edit the document properties through the document reference, by right-clicking the reference and selecting the Properties option. The document properties dialog box is shown in Figure 9.9.

As shown in Figure 9.9, there are five categories of document properties: Document, Version, Sharing, Activity Log, and Personalize. The most common document properties and their descriptions are listed in Table 9.4.

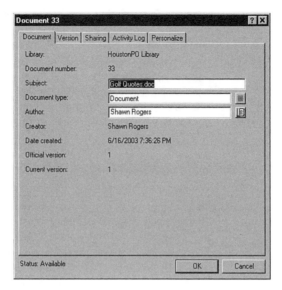

FIGURE 9.9
Use the document properties dialog box to obtain details about a document in a GroupWise library.

TABLE 9.4 Document Properties

PROPERTY	DESCRIPTION
Library	The library that contains the document.
Document Number	A number assigned by GroupWise that is used by the document management system to identify the document.
Subject	A text field that enables you to assign a descriptive subject for the document, such as "1996 Annual Report." When you import documents, you have the option to make the filename and path the document subject. Otherwise, you can specify the subject as you create the document, or you can edit the subject in the properties dialog box.
Document Type	A classification for the document that is used to categorize and establish the usage of the document. For example, some common document types include Agenda, Contract, Memo, Minutes, Proposal, and Report. These classifications, or

TABLE 9.4 Continued

PROPERTY	DESCRIPTION
	types, facilitate searches for specific documents. An important field in Document Type is the expiration setting. The expiration setting determines when a document expires and what should be done with the document when it expires.
Author	The author of the document. The author is not always the same as the creator. The author can be any GroupWise user.
Creator	The person who placed the document in the library.
Date Created	The date and time the document was placed in the library. (Note: If you imported the document from a file system, the date and time stamp on the file is not preserved in the document properties.)
Official Version	The version of the document that will be identified and viewed through searches. For example, if seven versions of the annual report were stored in the library, and version 6 was designated as the official version, it would be the version found in searches by GroupWise users who have View rights to the library. (Version 7 could be a draft in progress that is not yet ready for official release.) Any version of a document can be identified as the official version. If you do not specify an official version, the current version is the official version. Usually the creator of the document designates the official version, but the right to set the official version can be granted to others.
Current Version	GroupWise document management services allow up to 100 versions of a document. The current version is the latest version of the document.
Description	A text field that enables you to describe the current version of the document. By default, the description for the first version of a document will be "Original."
Status	The document status possibilities include "Available" (the document is available to be opened or checked out of the library), "In Use"

TABLE 9.4 Continued

PROPERTY	DESCRIPTION
	(another user currently has the document opened or checked out), and "Checked-Out" (another user has checked out the document).
Sharing	Shows the GroupWise users with whom you have shared the documents. You control the sharing properties for the documents you add to the library. By default, a document is not shared and cannot be accessed by other users. Sharing documents is discussed later in this chapter. (Note: The rights you specify for shared documents apply to all versions of the document.)
Activity Log	The Activity Log property shows you a chronological log of the actions that have been performed on the document, such as who created the document, who has opened the document, who has viewed the document, and who has edited the document.
Personalize	Lets you apply a predefined category type to a document. This feature is new to GroupWise 6.5.

NOTE You must have the Edit right to the library to change a document's properties. You likely have this right for your documents, but you may not have this right for public documents, depending on the library configuration set by your administrator.

Setting Default Document Properties

You can set default properties that will be used for all documents you import or create. To set default document properties, follow these steps:

1. Select Tools, Options.

2. Double-click the Documents icon.

3. Highlight the library you are using and click the Properties button.

4. In the property-configuration dialog box, shown in Figure 9.10, select the document property fields that you want available for your documents by default.

5. In the Document Defaults tab, you can specify a default document subject, document type, and author.

216

6. In the Sharing Defaults tab, you can set default sharing options. This is useful if you want all the documents you add to the library to be shared with others by default.

TIP If you are collaborating with others in a workgroup, you can use this sharing feature to specify all the other GroupWise users who should have access to your documents.

7. Choose OK when you're finished setting default document properties.

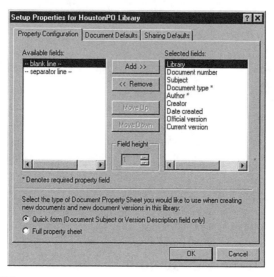

FIGURE 9.10
Set default document properties with the Setup Properties dialog box.

The values you set become the default properties for any documents you create or import in the library.

Using Find

In Chapter 5, "Message Management," we discussed how to use the Find feature. This chapter discusses how to perform a full text search to find items, including documents that contain specific words or phrases. The Advanced Find options are very useful for searching document libraries.

NOTE When you use the Find feature, GroupWise searches for your document in the default library first.

To find a document using Standard Find options, follow these steps:

1. Select Tools, Find.

2. Select the Find tab.

3. Specify a full text search or a subject line search.

4. Type the word or words you want to find in the text box.

5. (Optional) Specify either From/Author or To/CC.

6. (Optional) Specify the item type you want to search for, such as email or document.

7. (Optional) Specify the item source, such as received or posted.

8. (Optional) Specify a date range to search.

9. Specify the folders to search by clicking the boxes next to these folders.

10. Click OK to perform the search.

TIP You can expand the Mailbox to select individual folders or click the All Libraries icon to select individual libraries.

GroupWise performs the search and returns a list of documents or messages that meet your specified search criteria.

Here's how to find a document using Advanced Find options:

1. Select Tools, Find.

2. Select the Find tab.

3. Click the Advanced Find button.

4. Specify the Find criteria using the Advanced Find dialog box. Figure 9.11 shows how to find all entries where the author is Kellie Rogers, the library is Houston-Sales, and the subject contains the word *golf*.

5. Click OK to accept the advanced search criteria.

6. Specify any additional search options and click OK to begin the search.

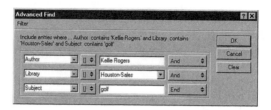

FIGURE 9.11
Use Advanced Find to specify detailed search options.

GroupWise presents you with a list of the documents that met the search criteria.

Sharing Documents

When you place documents in a library, you control who has access to those documents through the Sharing tab of the document properties dialog box. You also control what rights others have to the document.

Here's how to share a document with other users:

1. Right-click the document reference in your Mailbox and choose Properties.

2. Click the Sharing tab. The dialog box shown in Figure 9.12 displays. The default sharing property is Not shared. Not shared means that no other GroupWise user has access to the document. Notice that GroupWise inserts General User Access and Creator Access in the Share list. By default, general users (all users with access to the library) do not have any rights to the document, and the author/creator has full rights to the document.

3. Click the Shared with option.

4. Type the username in the Name field and click Add User. Alternatively, you can click the Address Selector button and double-click the users' names in the address list. The names appear in the Share list window.

By default, the new users have the View right, which means that the users can locate the document in searches and can view the document, but they cannot modify it.

FIGURE 9.12
Use the Sharing tab to grant other users access to your documents in the library.

NOTE The rights you specify are for all versions of a document. If you want to specify different rights for each version of a document, click the Version Level Security button.

To specify additional rights, follow these steps:

1. Highlight the user in the Share list window.

2. Click the check boxes for Edit, Delete, Share, or Modify security to grant those rights. Table 9.5 lists the user rights options for a document.

TABLE 9.5   User Rights Options for a Document

RIGHT	DESCRIPTION
Edit	Users can make changes to the document.
Delete	Users can delete the document. Use this right with care.
Share	Users can add the document to shared folders, thereby sharing the document with other GroupWise users.

TABLE 9.5 Continued

RIGHT	DESCRIPTION
Modify Security	Users can modify the rights for the document. If you grant this right, the users can modify the other rights and could grant themselves the Edit and Delete rights.

Use the General User Access entry to grant the same rights to all users who have access to the library. For example, if for some reason you want everyone to be able to delete the file, highlight General User Access and grant the Delete right.

> **NOTE** A user must have the Edit and View rights before he or she can have the Modify security right.

When you grant users the Edit or Delete right, GroupWise automatically gives them View rights to the document. Without the View right, a user cannot see the document in the results of a Find operation, in shared folders, and so on.

When you grant other users rights to the document, the users do not automatically receive a document reference in their Mailboxes. They can only access the document by using Find.

Typically, you grant rights to a document, and those rights apply to all versions of that document. However, you can use the Version Security option to specify rights only to a specific version of a document.

Set security on a specific version of a document by following these steps:

1. Right-click a document and select Properties.
2. Click the Sharing tab.
3. If necessary, add a user as instructed previously.
4. Highlight the user in the Share List window.
5. Click the Version Level Security button.
6. Enable the specific rights for this version by placing a check in the appropriate check box, as shown in Figure 9.13.
7. Click OK to close the Version Level Security dialog box.
8. Click OK to close the document properties dialog box.

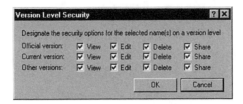

FIGURE 9.13
The Sharing feature lets you specify security at the document version level.

The users to whom you granted rights will now be able to perform additional operations on the document.

Using the Find Results Folders with Document Management

The GroupWise Find Results Folder feature is very powerful when combined with the GroupWise document management capabilities. You can create folders that allow you to display only documents that have specific properties.

A common use of these folders is to display the document references of all the documents you have stored in the library or to create folders that contain the document references of specific document types, such as contracts.

To create a Find Results Folder that displays all your documents, follow these steps:

1. Right-click your Cabinet or a folder and select New Folder.

2. Select the Find Results Folder type.

3. Select the Custom Find Results Folder option and click Next.

4. Give the folder a name.

5. (Optional) Give the folder a description.

6. Click Next.

7. In the Create Find Results Folder dialog box, select only Document as the item type.

8. Enter your name in the From/Author field.

9. In the right pane, specify which libraries should be searched.

10. Set any other options you desire, such as a date range.

11. Click Next.

12. (Optional) Change the View By, Sort By, and Sort Order settings so the items display according to your personal preference.

13. (Optional) Select your desired item source.

14. Select only Document as the item type.

15. (Optional) Edit the columns that should display when the folder is accessed.

16. Click Finish.

This folder will now display all the library documents you have authored.

Performing Mass Document Operations

GroupWise document management services let you perform operations on many documents at once by using the Mass Document Operations option. With this option, you can perform these operations on several documents at once:

- ▶ Change document properties
- ▶ Move
- ▶ Delete
- ▶ Change sharing
- ▶ Copy

NOTE A system administrator can grant a GroupWise user "manage" rights. If you have received manage rights to a library, you have additional capabilities available to you when performing mass document operations. For information on the actions you can perform with the manage rights, refer to the GroupWise Help feature.

For example, if you need to move or copy a large number of documents from one GroupWise library to another, you should use the Mass Document Operations option.

To use the Mass Document Operations option, follow these steps:

1. (Optional) In your GroupWise Mailbox, highlight the documents on which you want to perform the operation.

2. Select Tools, Mass Document Operations. The dialog box in Figure 9.14 displays.

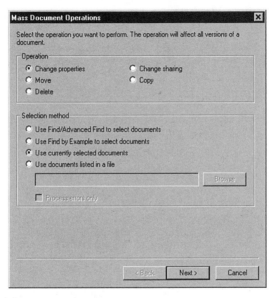

FIGURE 9.14
Use the Mass Document Operations dialog box to manipulate many library documents at once.

3. Select the desired operation: Change properties, Move, Delete, Change sharing, or Copy.

4. Choose your selection method.

5. Click Next.

Follow the prompts to perform the operation. (The prompts will vary depending on the type of operation you are performing.)

Echoing Documents to Your Remote Mailbox

If you use the remote features of GroupWise (discussed in the next chapter), you can "echo" documents from your default library to a library created in your remote mailbox, which is located on your hard drive.

This feature lets you work on documents that are stored in the library locally while you are not connected to your master GroupWise mailbox. This feature maintains two copies of your documents—one in the library and one in your GroupWise remote mailbox stored on your local hard drive.

When you reconnect, you can then update the documents you have modified.

Here's how to enable document echoing:

1. Select Tools, Options.
2. Double-click the Documents icon.
3. Select the General tab.
4. Choose the Echo documents to GroupWise remote option.
5. Click OK.

Documents will be echoed to your remote mailbox any time you close or check in a document in your master mailbox. A document reference is created for the echoed document in your remote mailbox.

Summary

This chapter explained the basics of GroupWise document management and GroupWise libraries, including accessing GroupWise libraries, importing documents, working with documents in a GroupWise library, setting security options on documents, and deleting documents.

In the next chapter we explain how to use GroupWise Remote Mode to remain connected while you are away from the office.

CHAPTER 10

Remote Access

With today's mobile workforce, access to email and scheduling information is more critical than ever. If you can access your messaging system regardless of where you are, you can communicate with your customers and co-workers as if you were sitting in your office.

One way to access your GroupWise system when you are away from the office is to use the GroupWise client running in Remote Mode. This chapter addresses how to configure the GroupWise client for remote access. We explain the steps necessary to access information when you're out of the office—how to request your messages and how to connect to the system and download your messages. We also explain the different techniques to use when you are connected to a network and when you are working offline using a remote mailbox.

NOTE In addition to the traditional Remote Mode, GroupWise 6.5 has a hybrid mode known as *Caching Mode* that functions similar to the standard Online Mode but has some Remote Mode characteristics. When you use Caching Mode, you won't notice much difference between the standard Online Mode and the Caching Mode, except perhaps a slight delay in sending and receiving messages. This mode is discussed in this chapter also.

Using GroupWise Remote Mode is just one way to access your GroupWise information when you aren't directly connected to the network. You can use GroupWise WebAccess to access your GroupWise account from any Internet connection. GroupWise WebAccess is explained in Chapter 12, "Mobile GroupWise Access."

Connecting to Your Mailbox Using Remote Mode

You have three options to connect to your GroupWise Mailbox using Remote Mode:

- ▶ **Modem**—Using a dial-up connection to the GroupWise Async Gateway, which forwards your incoming and outgoing messages.

- ▶ **Network**—Using a drive letter and path to your post office on a network, possibly achieved through a dial-in, network-connection software package such as NetWare Connect.

- ▶ **TCP/IP**—Using the TCP/IP address of the GroupWise Mail server that synchronizes your master Mailbox with your remote Mailbox.

Traditionally, the most common method of connecting remotely to a GroupWise mailbox has been to use a dial-up connection through a modem. However, with broadband network access becoming more commonplace, TCP/IP connections are increasingly popular. All three types of connections will be explained in this chapter.

NOTE Before configuring GroupWise in Remote Mode, you must make sure you are running GroupWise from your local hard drive. In some installations, the GroupWise client might run from a network location. If you are unsure about the location of the GroupWise program, contact your system administrator.

Configuring the GroupWise Client

Two ways exist for beginning the configuration of Remote Mode. We suggest that you configure Remote Mode when you are connected to the network, if possible, because the procedure is automated. You will likely be able to use this method if you have a laptop computer that you use in a docking station when you are in the office and outside of the docking station while away from the office.

Configuring GroupWise Remote When Attached to the Network

To begin installing GroupWise in Remote Mode (assuming you are logged in to the network), follow these steps:

1. Click Tools, Hit the Road.

2. If you don't have a password on your master Mailbox, you will get a warning dialog box explaining that a password must be set. Click OK and GroupWise lets you set a password by presenting the Security Options dialog box. After you set your password, click Next. The Hit the Road Wizard starts.

3. Select This Machine and click Next.

4. Enter a local path for GroupWise to use for Remote Mode (for example, `c:\gwremote`). If the directory you specify does not exist, GroupWise will create it for you. Click Next.

5. Click Yes if you're prompted to create the folder.

6. In the GroupWise Async Gateway box, select the gateway your computer will use for Remote Mode. (If no numbers display, click Next and you will be able to enter the number later.)

7. In the Update Your Remote Mailbox screen, shown in Figure 10.1, select the items you want available to you when you are working remotely.

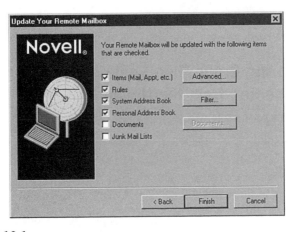

FIGURE 10.1
Use the Update Your Remote Mailbox screen to select which types of GroupWise items you want to have available while you're working offline in Remote Mode.

8. Click Finish.

9. If you get a prompt asking you if you want to use your master Mailbox password to access your remote Mailbox, choose Yes or No, depending on your preference. If you answer yes, you will be prompted to enter your password when you launch GroupWise in Remote Mode. We recommend you answer yes in case an unauthorized user gets access to your computer.

10. After you answer the password prompt, the GroupWise client will access your post office and download your Mailbox information to the Remote directory on your computer. You will see the dialog box shown in Figure 10.2.

FIGURE 10.2
The Updating Mailbox dialog box shows you the progress of the remote Mailbox update process.

You are now ready to use GroupWise in Remote Mode.

Configuring GroupWise Remote When Disconnected from the Network

These instructions make two assumptions:

▶ That you have already installed the GroupWise client locally on your computer

▶ That you or your system administrator have set a password on your master Mailbox and you know that password

If either of these assumptions is not valid, contact your system administrator before configuring GroupWise in Remote Mode.

NOTE To accomplish these steps, you will need to know the name of your GroupWise domain and post office. You can get this information from your system administrator.

To begin the configuration process, follow these steps:

1. Double-click the GroupWise icon or click Start, Programs, GroupWise, GroupWise. The GroupWise Startup screed will display. (The GroupWise Startup screen is explained in Appendix A, "GroupWise Startup Options.")

2. Enter your GroupWise user ID in the User ID field.

3. Enter the password for your master Mailbox in the Password field.

4. Click the Remote Mailbox Path option.

5. Enter a local path for GroupWise Remote, such as `c:\GWRemote`.

6. If you are prompted to create the directory, select Yes.

7. Click OK. GroupWise starts and prompts you to create an account.

8. Click OK. The Create Account dialog box displays, as shown in Figure 10.3.

FIGURE 10.3
Use the Create Account dialog box to set up Remote Mode while offline.

9. Enter the name you'll use for the account.

10. Select GroupWise in the Account type field.

11. Click Next. The Create GroupWise Account dialog box displays, as shown in Figure 10.4.

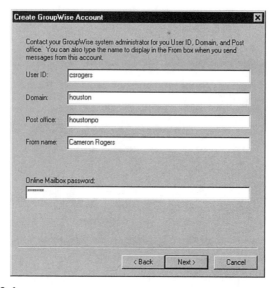

FIGURE 10.4
Enter your GroupWise system information in the Create GroupWise Account dialog box.

12. Enter your GroupWise user ID in the User ID field.

13. Enter the name of your GroupWise domain in the Domain field.

14. Enter the name of your GroupWise post office in the Post office field.

15. Enter your full name in the From name field. (This is the name that will appear on mail messages you send from GroupWise Remote.)

16. Enter your GroupWise password in the Online Mailbox password field.

17. Click Next. The Create GroupWise Account dialog box displays.

18. Select the appropriate location in the Connecting from field. (Default Location is fine if no other locations are configured.)

19. Click the Connect To button. The Create Connection dialog box displays, as shown in Figure 10.5.

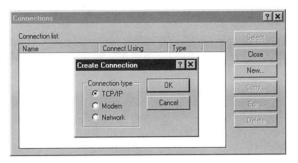

FIGURE 10.5
Use the Create Connection dialog box to specify the type of connection you will use with GroupWise Remote.

20. Select Modem, OK. The Modem Connection dialog box displays, as shown in Figure 10.6.

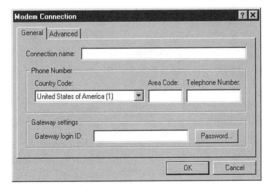

FIGURE 10.6
The Modem Connection dialog box.

21. Enter a recognizable name in the Connection name field, such as GroupWise Remote Connection.

NOTE Steps 22 through 25 require information that must be obtained from your system administrator or help desk.

22. In the Phone Number area, enter the area code and phone number of the GroupWise Async Gateway.

23. In the Gateway settings area, enter the gateway login ID in the appropriate field.

24. Click the Password button, enter the gateway password, and click OK. Then reenter the gateway password to confirm it and click OK again.

25. Click OK in the Modem Connection dialog box.

26. In the Connection dialog box, highlight the connection you just created and click Select.

27. Click Finish in the Create GroupWise Account dialog box. You are asked if you want to use your online Mailbox password to access your remote Mailbox. Select Yes if you want to protect your remote Mailbox with your password; otherwise, select No.

GroupWise is now configured to run in Remote Mode with a modem connection.

Setting Up TCP/IP Connections

GroupWise remote connections using TCP/IP are popular because they can "share" the TCP/IP connection (whether LAN or dial-up) you might be using for Web browsing.

With a TCP/IP remote connection, you can connect to your GroupWise Mailbox through the Internet. If your system allows you to use TCP/IP connections to connect to your Mailbox, you should use this method.

TCP/IP connections use an IP address and port to connect to your master GroupWise system. To configure a TCP/IP connection, follow steps 1–19 in the previous section and then select TCP/IP as the connection type. The TCP/IP Connection dialog box will display, as shown in Figure 10.7.

Enter a connection name, IP address, and IP port and then click OK. You can then use this connection to send and receive messages in Remote Mode.

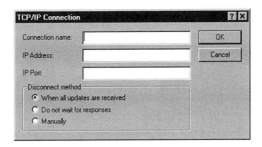

FIGURE 10.7
Use the TCP/IP Connection dialog box to configure a remote TCP/IP connection to your master Mailbox.

Setting Up Network Connections

A network connection lets you connect directly with your main GroupWise system through the network. This connection is used most often by people who travel to a branch office with a wide area network (WAN) link to the network.

All you need to know to use a network connection is the proper drive letter and a path to your GroupWise post office.

To configure a network connection, follow steps 1–19 in the previous section and then select Network as the connection type. The Network Connection dialog box will display, as shown in Figure 10.8.

TIP If you are using GroupWise on the network, among the information in the Help, About GroupWise box is the path (drive letter and directory) of your post office. You can use this information to enter the path in the Network Connection dialog box.

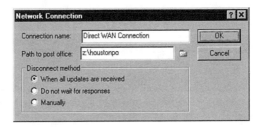

FIGURE 10.8
Use the Network Connection dialog box to create a remote connection over a WAN link.

To create a network connection, simply enter a name for the connection and the path to the post office.

Modifying Your GroupWise Remote Options

After GroupWise is configured on your remote computer, a new icon labeled Accounts (Remote) is available in the Tools, Options menu. This icon is used to set default parameters for GroupWise Remote operations. When you double-click this icon, you see the Accounts dialog box, shown in Figure 10.9.

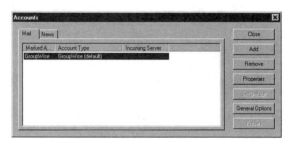

FIGURE 10.9
Use the Accounts (Remote) options to establish GroupWise Remote parameters.

From the Accounts dialog box, you can click Properties to modify the connection properties for GroupWise Remote. You can also click General Options to force GroupWise to dial up and synchronize with the master Mailbox on given intervals.

The important options you can configure in the Properties screen are explained in Table 10.1.

TABLE 10.1 GroupWise Remote Connection Properties

PROPERTY	EXPLANATION
Time Zone (located under the Server tab)	GroupWise needs to know the time zone where you reside so it can automatically adjust appointment times. This setting is important if you live in a time zone different from the time zone where your master GroupWise system is located. GroupWise

TABLE 10.1 Continued

PROPERTY	EXPLANATION
	automatically adjusts the appointments you create depending on the time zone information that is entered here.
Delete Options (located under the Advanced tab)	The Delete Options tab lets you configure the synchronization of deleted messages between your master and remote Mailbox. The options at the top of the dialog box let you specify what happens to messages in your master Mailbox when you delete messages from your remote Mailbox (and vice versa). The Always Delete option automatically deletes messages from your master Mailbox (a deletion request will be sent to the server the next time the client connects). The Never Delete option indicates that messages from your master Mailbox are not to be deleted. The Prompt Me option asks you what to do with the master Mailbox each time you delete a message from your remote Mailbox.
Item Downloads (located under the Advanced tab)	Specifies which items to download when you connect.
Item Downloads (located under the Advanced tab, Advanced button)	Lets you set date ranges for items you want to download from your master Mailbox.

NOTE The selections you make in the Tools, Options, Accounts (Remote) menus are system defaults. You can override the default options during a specific connection if you desire.

Using GroupWise in Remote Mode

Very few functional differences exist between using GroupWise Remote and using GroupWise while logged in to the network (Online Mode). The same set of program files are used, the screens all look the same, and you access all your information the same way.

When you use GroupWise in Online Mode, you are working directly with your master Mailbox, which is stored on the network. When you leave the office and need to use GroupWise, the program will use a remote version of your Mailbox, which is stored on the computer you are using remotely. The messages and Calendar items you create in Remote Mode are stored in the remote Mailbox until you connect to the GroupWise system and synchronize the two Mailboxes.

You must remember to reestablish a connection from the Remote client to your master Mailbox after you use GroupWise Remote so that the master Mailbox will be updated with the latest information.

Introducing the Remote Menu

One of the most noticeable differences between GroupWise running in the standard network mode and GroupWise Remote Mode is a new menu item called Accounts. The following selections are available from the Accounts menu:

▶ **Send/Retrieve, <Remote Account Name>**—Here, you can configure and initiate the remote connection. (The remote account name is the name you specified previously for your GroupWise remote account.)

▶ **Send/Retrieve, GroupWise Options**—Here, you can specify which items you want to download during the connection.

▶ **Pending Requests**—Used to view and manage requests waiting to be uploaded and responded to by the master system. Usually, you won't need to do anything in this screen.

▶ **Connection Log**—Used to view the connection details in the log file. You can also see this information if you click the Show Log button when you make a connection to the master system.

▶ **Show Status Window**—Displays the connection status window.

▶ **Auto Send/Retrieve**—This is a toggle setting that turns off the automatic send/retrieve mode. This mode is configured under Account Options, General Options. This mode is also known as *Synchronized Mode*. When this option is enabled, GroupWise automatically uploads and downloads on a specified interval.

The Accounts menu will also display when you are running in Caching Mode (explained later in this chapter), but it will not display when you're running in Online Mode.

Sending Messages

For the most part, there is not much difference between using GroupWise remotely and using it on the network: You use the Address Book (and Address Selector) and send messages, create Calendar entries, and reply to and forward messages the same way. The only difference is that you need to connect to the master system to actually send messages.

Busy Search

Busy Search is slightly different if you are in Remote Mode. When you are creating an appointment while you are out of the office, you might not want to wait until the appointment request has been received (and either accepted or declined) by the people you need at the meeting. If you need faster information about whether the invitees are available for an appointment, set up Busy Search in the normal way. (See Chapter 7, "Group Calendaring and Task Management," for a complete discussion of Busy Search on the network.)

Once you have configured the Appointment information for the Busy Search, choose to connect now or wait until the next time you connect to send the Busy Search request to the GroupWise system, as shown in Figure 10.10. Either way, you will receive the results of your Busy Search, and you can continue creating your appointment request.

TIP You should save the incomplete appointment in the Work In Progress folder while you are waiting for the outcome of the Busy Search. When the results arrive, open the draft appointment, complete the information, and choose Send. Don't forget to connect again to actually send the message to the system. If you are running in the synchronized mode (that is, Auto Send/Retrieve is turned on), the Busy Search happens during the automatic synchronization process.

Connecting to the Master System

GroupWise Remote Mode is a *request-based system*, which means that you work offline reading messages, creating new appointments, and making other changes to your remote Mailbox. Once you have made all your changes and are ready to connect to the main system, you will generate a list of requests for items.

One request will be to send out all your outgoing messages. Another request will be to retrieve your new messages, sent to you since the last time you connected to the main GroupWise system. You can make other requests (for example, to get a new copy of the Address Book). When you connect using any of the methods listed in the previous section, your requests are transferred to the main GroupWise system.

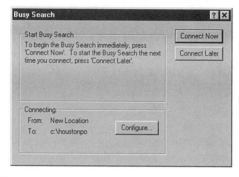

FIGURE 10.10

The Busy Search option lets you generate an immediate request for free/busy information from GroupWise users when scheduling an appointment.

The GroupWise system generates responses to your requests, compresses them, and transfers them via your connection to your remote computer. Some of your requests will be handled in the same session in which you sent them (to get your new messages, for example), and others are transferred the next time you connect.

Once the request list has been completed, the connection is terminated, and the responses are decompressed and added to your remote Mailbox.

To request items, follow these steps:

1. Choose Accounts, Send/Retrieve, GroupWise Options. The dialog box shown in Figure 10.11 displays.

2. If you would like to refine your request for items to a specific set of items or a specific time range, click the Advanced button to display the dialog box shown in Figure 10.12. Choose the options you want from the following tabs:

   ▶ **Retrieve**—Lets you configure the date range from which GroupWise will retrieve messages. The default is 5 days prior to the current day. If you have not connected in several days, you may need to increase this range. You can also choose the Retrieve all changes since I last connected option.

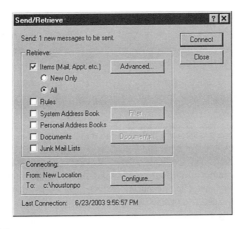

FIGURE 10.11
Use the Send/Retrieve dialog box to update your remote Mailbox with
information from your master Mailbox.

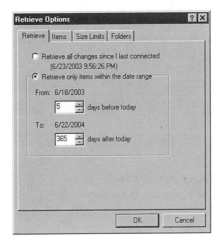

FIGURE 10.12
Use the Retrieve Options dialog box to refine your remote Mailbox update
request.

▶ **Items**—Lets you select what message categories you want to
update (Mail and Phone, Appointments, and so on) and set
up a filter to retrieve specific messages matching certain
criteria (for example, messages that contain "Miller Project" in
the subject).

▶ **Size Limits**—Lets you retrieve messages that fall into a specific size range. (For example, you may choose to only retrieve messages with attachments that are less than 30KB in size.) You can also retrieve just the subject line and then get the message information later. This feature can be very useful to minimize connection time and phone charges.

TIP If you are reading a message that has been truncated due to size limitations, you can select Accounts, Retrieve Item, and the entire message will be downloaded during your next remote connection. If you have several messages in your Mailbox that have been truncated due to file size limits, use Ctrl+click to select each message in the main GroupWise screen and then click Accounts, Retrieve Selected Items. The complete messages will be downloaded during your next connection.

▶ **Folders**—Lets you select the folders you want updated. You can use this feature in conjunction with the Rules feature to move only those messages you want retrieved to a certain Remote folder so that you can simply download messages from this folder. The Folders feature makes the remote connection more efficient. Simply click the box next to the folder to select it for updating.

3. Click OK to return to the Send/Retrieve dialog box.

4. Make other selections from the Send/Retrieve dialog box, as desired:

▶ **Rules**—Updates all rules between the remote and master Mailboxes.

▶ **System Address Book**—Updates your remote Mailbox with the most current Address Book. Click Filter to select which address book you want (your Post Office or Domain address book).

▶ **Personal Address Book**—Synchronizes your master and remote personal address books.

▶ **Documents**—Lets you select the documents you want to retrieve if you have GroupWise Document Management Services enabled on your system. You can select documents from their folders, and the documents will be transferred to your Mailbox. See Chapter 9, "Document Management," for more information about document management.

> ▶ **Junk Mail Lists**—Lets you download to your remote mail-
> box the list of junk mail addresses you have configured for
> your master Mailbox.

5. Verify that the connection you want to use appears at the bottom of
   the dialog box. If you need to change the connection, click the
   Configure button and set up the desired connection. See the sec-
   tions earlier in this chapter on setting up TCP/IP and network connections for more information.

Choose Connect to complete the request and connect to the master system. To see the details of the connection, click the Show Log button. The
Connection Log dialog box, shown in Figure 10.13, displays the session
information and can be helpful in troubleshooting. This information is
saved to a log file and can be accessed from the Connection Log option
under the Accounts menu.

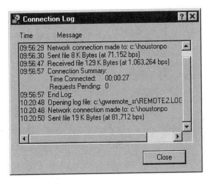

FIGURE 10.13
The Connection Log dialog box shows the connection activity and is useful
when troubleshooting remote connection difficulties.

Understanding Hit the Road

One of the easiest features of GroupWise is also probably the most useful
feature for remote users. Hit the Road is a one-step way to update your
remote Mailbox before you leave the office.

The Hit the Road feature is used while you are connected to the network
and directly accessing your master Mailbox. As your final preparation for
leaving the office, you use the Hit the Road feature to do a last-minute

synchronization of your remote Mailbox. This prevents a long connection during your first GroupWise remote connection after leaving the office.

TIP If you use Hit the Road while connected to the network, a network connection is created automatically. You won't have to manually enter the network connection information discussed earlier.

The instructions in this section assume that you have already configured your system to use GroupWise in Remote Mode.

To use Hit the Road, follow these steps:

1. While logged in to GroupWise on the network, finish all messaging transactions (replies, new messages, and so on).

2. Choose Tools, Hit the Road.

3. When prompted, enter the password for your Mailbox in the dialog box.

4. Select which items you want to be updated to your remote Mailbox this time by Hit the Road. You can configure the items each time you use Hit the Road.

NOTE If you would like to customize your items choices, click the Advanced button and make the appropriate selections.

5. You can choose which address book you need to use by clicking the Filter button next to the System Address Book item. Select any of the items in the list to limit your Address Book as you like.

6. If GroupWise Document Management is set up on your system, you can also select the documents you need by clicking the box next to Documents. You can then select the documents you need by clicking the Documents button and making your selections.

7. Click Finish. This action will initiate a network connection to your post office, and the items you selected are downloaded into your remote Mailbox.

You are now ready to "hit the road."

NOTE You will see two or three extra windows open and close automatically while the synchronization takes place. If you want more information about what is happening, click the Show Log button of the Network Connection dialog box.

Understanding Smart Docking

Suppose you are using a notebook computer and have been away on a business trip. When you come back into the office after using GroupWise Remote, any changes you have made while on the road since your last connection can be automatically updated to your master Mailbox on the network. This feature is known as *Smart Docking*.

When you start GroupWise the first time after being off of the network, GroupWise automatically synchronizes the changes in your remote Mailbox with your master Mailbox. Because the connection type— modem or logged in to the network—is sensed automatically, no configuration is necessary.

> **NOTE** If you select the Don't Display This Prompt Again message, the Mailbox will be updated without any user intervention.

With the Smart Docking feature of GroupWise, you don't need to worry about how you are connected to GroupWise; the program will keep your master Mailbox synchronized with changes made in your remote Mailbox. Of course, to get the updates from your master Mailbox to your remote Mailbox, you need to use the Hit the Road feature, as discussed previously.

Understanding Caching Mode

A new GroupWise operating mode was introduced with GroupWise 6.0, know as *Caching Mode*. (This mode was not available in GroupWise versions prior to 6.0.) This mode is a cross between the standard Online Mode (live connection to your master Mailbox) and the Remote Mode discussed in this chapter.

The Caching Mode is similar to Online Mode because it is commonly used while you are actually connected to the network. The difference between the Online and Caching Modes is that when you are using Online Mode, you are maintaining a live connection to your GroupWise master Mailbox. This mode uses GroupWise system resources even when you are not performing tasks in GroupWise. In some cases, this mode can stress the GroupWise delivery mechanism by creating unnecessary network and GroupWise traffic.

If you are running in Caching Mode, the messages you send to other users are temporarily queued in a directory on your local hard drive (just like in Remote Mode). Likewise, messages sent to you from other users are temporarily queued at your GroupWise post office. At regular intervals, your GroupWise client automatically initiates a connection to your post office and uploads any messages you have created and downloads any messages that have been sent to you.

NOTE Your GroupWise system administrator can force your GroupWise client to run in Caching Mode to more effectively manage system resources.

You can tell whether you are running in Caching Mode by looking at the status indicator in the upper-left corner of the main GroupWise screen.

Summary

The GroupWise Remote features described in this chapter allow you to work with your GroupWise information when you are away from the office and need to access your Mailbox through an Internet connection, a WAN link, or a telephone line.

The next chapter will explain how to customize GroupWise to match your personal preferences and work style.

CHAPTER 11

Customizing GroupWise

GroupWise enables you to customize your environment to reflect personal work style and preferences. In this chapter we explain the options for customizing your GroupWise environment.

Often, you can select options to override the defaults you set. For example, you may decide to set your default message priority level to Normal. When you want to send a high-priority message, you can change the priority level to High for that particular message (without changing the default). The next message you create will again use the default, Normal-priority level, unless you decide to override the default again.

GroupWise 6.5 has the powerful capability of using certificates to encrypt and digitally sign messages. We discuss how to set up this option in this chapter.

Also in this chapter we explain how to set GroupWise default options, how to customize the Toolbar, and how to customize your folders.

Setting Default Options

When you click Tools, Options from the main GroupWise menu, you see the dialog box shown in Figure 11.1. Use this dialog box to set your GroupWise default options (in other words, your preferences).

FIGURE 11.1
These applets let you set the defaults for GroupWise.

You can set defaults for the GroupWise environment (that is, the overall program interface) for sending messages, document management, security, certificates, and the Calendar. If you are running GroupWise in Remote Mode (discussed in Chapter 10, "Remote Access"), you will also have a "Remote" option.

NOTE The default settings for document management (the settings that correspond to the Documents icon in the Options dialog box) are explained in Chapter 9, "Document Management."

Environment Options

The Environment preferences group enables you to modify characteristics of the overall GroupWise program interface. When you double-click the Environment icon, you see a dialog box with six (seven in Remote Mode) tabs: General, Views, File Location, Cleanup, Default Actions, Signature, and Backup Options (Remote Mode only), as shown in Figure 11.2.

General

Under the General tab, you can set the following preferences:

▶ **Interface Language**—This is the language you want to use in the client interface (menus, views, and so on). If the language you desire does not appear, contact your system administrator. Languages are enabled at the system level.

▶ **View Options**—These options enable you to read the next message after you accept, decline, or delete a message and to open a new, blank message after you send a message.

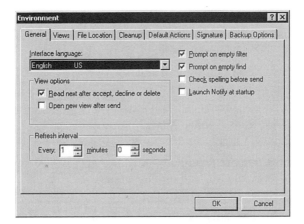

FIGURE 11.2
Environment options pertain to the overall default settings for GroupWise.

▶ **Refresh Interval**—This option determines how often GroupWise checks for new messages. (The minimum is 1 minute, the maximum is 60 minutes and 59 seconds, and the default is 1 minute.)

▶ **Prompt on Empty Filter**—This option causes a message to appear if a filter you created does not allow any messages to appear.

▶ **Prompt on Empty Find**—This option causes a message to appear if a Find session doesn't generate any results.

▶ **Check Spelling Before Send**—This option checks the spelling of each message (subject line and message body) when the Send or Post button is selected.

▶ **Launch Notify at Startup**—This option loads the Notify program, which will alert you to new messages and/or alarms set for appointments, when you start GroupWise.

Once you have set the General tab's options, you can select the Views tab's preferences.

Views

Under the Views tab, shown in Figure 11.3, you can set the following preferences:

▶ **Item Type**—Select the category (Mail, Phone, Reminder note, Appointment, Task, and Calendar) and the message type (Group or Posted) for which you want to set the default.

▶ **Views**—Choose from a list of available views for the selected item type.

▶ **Set Default View**—Highlight the view you want as the default for the item type you specify. (When you choose File, New, this is the view that will appear for the message type you choose.)

▶ **Default Compose/Read View**—Choose between plain text and HTML for composing and reading messages.

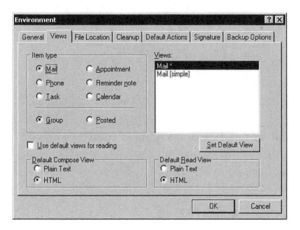

FIGURE 11.3
The Views tab's options configure the default views for sending and receiving messages.

NOTE The Calendar default view is the view that appears when you select the Calendar View option from the Window menu.

The Use default views for reading option enables you to read messages using your default views instead of the views the messages were sent with. For example, if someone sends you a Small Mail view message, you would normally see the message using the Small Mail view. However, if you marked the Use default views for reading check box, you see the message in whichever view you chose as the default.

File Location

Following are the preferences you can set under the File Location tab, which is shown in Figure 11.4:

▶ **Archive Directory**—The location of the parent directory of the actual archive directory that holds your archive message files. The system administrator may want you to place your archive files in a certain location.

▶ **Custom Views**—The location for Custom View files. (Custom views are specialized GroupWise views created with a view designer utility.)

▶ **Save, Check Out**—The default location for messages and attachments that you save, and the default location to place the documents that you check out of a GroupWise library. (See Chapter 9 for more information on using GroupWise libraries.)

▶ **Caching Mailbox Directory (Cache Mode only)**—This is the path to your cached Mailbox on your local computer. It is only available (obviously) in Caching Mode (see Chapter 10).

Once you have set up these file locations, you can configure the Cleanup tab's options.

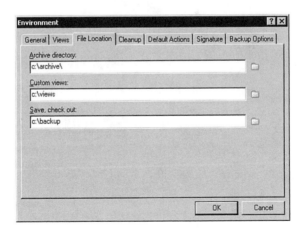

FIGURE 11.4
These fields allow you to specify default file locations for some elements of GroupWise.

Cleanup

Following are the preferences you can select under the Cleanup tab, which is shown in Figure 11.5:

▶ **Mail and Phone**—Specifies how old a phone or mail message will be when it is automatically archived or deleted. (The minimum is 1 day, the maximum is 250 days, and the default is Manual Delete and Archive.)

▶ **Appointment, Task, and Reminder Note**—Specifies how much past Calendar information you want to keep. (The minimum is 1 day, the maximum is 250 days, and the default is Manual Delete and Archive.)

▶ **Empty Trash**—Specifies how long any deleted item will stay in the Trash folder. (The minimum is 1 day, the maximum is 250 days, and the default is 7 days.) Once messages have been emptied from the Trash folder, they are no longer retrievable.

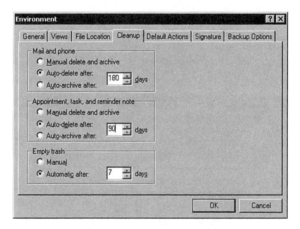

FIGURE 11.5
You can determine default actions to be taken based on the age of your messages.

The options in the Cleanup tab are performed when you start GroupWise. For example, if you have set Cleanup options so that messages are archived after 180 days, the archiving occurs when you start GroupWise on the 180th day after a message was received. The automatic Cleanup options can cause a slight delay when you start GroupWise.

Default Actions

The Default Actions tab, shown in Figure 11.6, lets you configure what happens when you access different items in GroupWise:

▶ **Sent Items**—These options specify what happens when you double-click a message you have sent. Open item opens the message, whereas Show properties displays the properties of the item.

▶ **Web Browser**—These options specify what happens when you click a Web page address within a message. Use existing window redirects your open Web browser to the address, whereas Open new window launches a new Web browser pointed to the address.

▶ **Show or Hide QuickViewer On**—These options let you configure what happens when you access QuickViewer (show or hide on all or selected folders or display a dialog box for a prompt).

▶ **File Attachments**—These options specify what happens when you click a file that is attached to a message. View in a new window opens a new message window displaying the contents of the file, whereas Open Attachment launches the application associated with the attached file.

▶ **Message Attachments**—These options specify what happens when you click a message that has been attached to an email. You can choose to view the attachment in either a new window by itself or within the same window of the message you are reading.

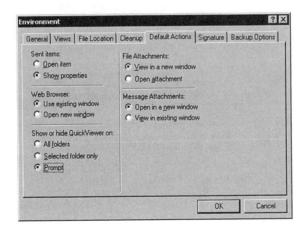

FIGURE 11.6
You can determine the default activities when accessing messages, Web addresses, and other items within the Default Actions tab.

Once you have set up the default actions, you can configure your signature.

Signature

You can enhance your GroupWise messages with an Internet-style, custom signature. The signature can be added to the end of any message you send. You can include information such as a disclaimer, an encouraging quotation, or your phone number. GroupWise also lets you send your own personal information (name, phone numbers, and so on) as they appear in the Address Book in the new vCard format. You can specify additional signature information for each mail account you are accessing with GroupWise. (This is covered in more detail in Chapter 8, "Advanced Features.")

To configure a signature or vCard sending options, click the Signature tab in the Environment dialog box, as shown in Figure 11.7.

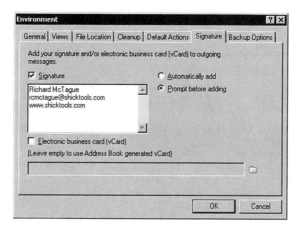

FIGURE 11.7
The Signature tab lets you configure your signature information for messages.

Following are the options available in the Signature tab:

▶ **Signature**—When you select this check box, you can type a signature in the Signature box as you want it to appear at the end of your messages.

▶ **Electronic Business Card (vCard)**—Enables the sharing of your personal information in the vCard (VCF) format. vCard is a format for contact information that is recognized by many Internet-based and other types of email systems. Sending a message with a vCard adds a VCF file as an attachment. The recipient then opens the attachment and specifies which address book to add the contact into. For example, if you send a vCard attachment to a GroupWise recipient, the contact information is added to that person's personal address book or Frequent Contact list. Specify the path to the vCard file in the path area at the bottom of the dialog box.

NOTE If you leave the path to the vCard file empty, the information that you send when you include a vCard signature (that is, attachment) is pulled from the GroupWise System address book, which is entered and created by the administrator.

▶ **Automatically Add**—Automatically adds the signature and/or vCard at the end of every message when you click Send.

▶ **Prompt Before Adding**—Asks whether you would like to add a signature and/or vCard information when you choose Send. (This is the default option.)

TIP You can copy text into the Clipboard from any application and place it in the Signature box. Graphics and other Rich Text Format (RTF) data cannot be used. Also, any text you enter will be preceded by two hard returns. This is helpful to know if you want your signature to appear with exactly one line between it and the last line of text in your message—in this case, don't end that last line with a hard return.

Backup Options (Remote Only)

The Backup Options tab lets you specify the directory (provided by the administrator) in order to back up your remote GroupWise Mailbox to a file location. Click Backup Remote Mailbox, enter the directory path, make a selection in the Backup Remote Mailbox Every # Days option, and click OK.

GroupWise will back up your remote Mailbox to the location you specify. Remember, this option is only available in Remote Mode.

Send Options

When you double-click the Send icon, you will see six tabs at the top of the Send Options dialog box: Send Options, Mail, Appointment, Task, Reminder Note, and Security (see Figure 11.8). Each tab contains customizable settings that affect the defaults for the messages you send.

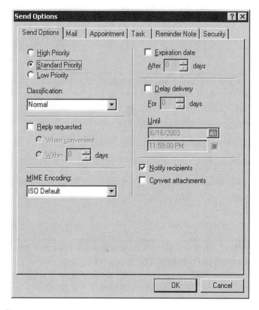

FIGURE 11.8
The main Send Options page lets you set defaults for all the messages you send.

The Send Options tab affects all messages (email, appointments, reminder notes, and tasks), and its options are explained in the following list:

▶ **Priority**—These options determine the default priority for each message type. High Priority means the message appears with a red icon in the recipient's Mailbox, and the message may be delivered more quickly by GroupWise. Standard Priority means the message appears with a regular icon in the Mailbox. Low Priority means the message appears with a dimmed icon in the Mailbox.

▶ **Classification**—These options place a security "header" at the top of the message body, such as "Security: For Your Eyes Only."

▶ **Reply Requested**—This option enables you to inform the recipient that you would like a reply to the message. When you set the Reply Requested option, GroupWise inserts text in the message body, stating that a reply is requested and how soon the reply is desired. The message icon shows two-way arrows, indicating that a reply is requested. When Convenient inserts "Reply Requested: When Convenient" in the message body, whereas Within X Days inserts "Reply Requested: By MM/DD/YY" in the message body.

▶ **MIME Encoding**—This is the encoding method for attachments sent to Internet recipients.

▶ **Expiration Date**—This option enables you to specify when the message will be automatically deleted from the recipient's Mailbox if the message is not opened.

▶ **Delay Delivery**—This option enables you to create a message now that will be sent after a specified number of days or on a certain date and time.

▶ **Notify Recipients**—This option specifies whether recipients receive a Notify message when the message arrives in their Mailboxes.

▶ **Convert Attachments**—This option specifies whether to convert attachments that are received through a gateway from another mail system. If the attachments are not converted, you will need the application with which the attachment was created to open it.

Now that these general send options are configured, you can set up default status tracking.

Status Tracking and Return Notification

The Mail tab, shown in Figure 11.9, along with the Appointment, Task, and Reminder Note tabs, enable you to configure the amount of status information and return notification available for each message you send. Following are the options available on these tabs:

▶ **Create a Sent Item to Track Information**—Specifies whether to create an entry in the Sent Items folder to track sent messages. Delivered shows you if and when the message was delivered to the recipient's Mailbox. Delivered and opened shows you when the message was delivered and when the message was opened. All information shows you all the aforementioned information, plus information about when the message was deleted, accepted, declined, and so on. Auto-delete sent item automatically removes the message from your Sent Items folder after all recipients have deleted the item and emptied it from their Trash folders.

▶ **Return Notification**—This option specifies an action that will automatically happen when the recipient opens, accepts, deletes, or completes a message or Calendar item. Mail Receipt means you'll receive an email message in your Mailbox informing you of the event. Notify means you'll receive an onscreen notification message informing you of the event. Notify and Mail means you receive both of these message types.

▶ **Internet Mail**—If you check this box, you can enable GroupWise to send an email when the receiving email system has successfully delivered the message. The receiving system needs to support this feature, known as *Extended SMTP (E-SMTP)*.

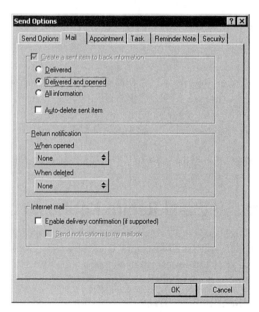

FIGURE 11.9
The Mail tab allows you to set up default options for status information and return notification for email messages.

The Appointment, Task, and Reminder Note tabs in the Send Options dialog box have the same configuration options as the Mail tab.

Security

GroupWise includes support for programs that encrypt and digitally sign messages. What is important to remember about message security is that the recipient must be able to understand and decrypt the messages you send.

NOTE The Security tab of the Send Options dialog box contains the same options as the Send tab of the Security Options dialog box. We will therefore cover them once.

You'll need to set up your certificates using the Certificates option, described in Chapter 8. The default security options in this tab, shown in Figure 11.10, enable advanced security for all the messages you send and are described as follows:

▶ **Conceal Subject**—This option prevents the message's subject line from appearing in the recipient's Mailbox. The subject line only appears when the recipient opens the item. Use this feature as an additional security measure when prying eyes may obtain information simply by seeing the subject line in the Mailbox.

▶ **Require Password to Complete Routed Item**—For messages that are sent sequentially using a routing slip (covered in Chapter 3, "Messaging Fundamentals"), each user will be required to enter his or her GroupWise password to mark it "Completed."

NOTE The other security options on the Security tab of the Send Options dialog box enable you to configure the encryption and digital signatures of your messages. These options are only available if you have previously installed an encryption program that is GroupWise enabled.

▶ **Select a Security Service Provider**—Either the Microsoft Enhanced Cryptographic Provider or Basic Cryptography Provider can be selected.

▶ **Secure Item Options**—Using S/MIME, this option enables you to encrypt the contents of a message and/or digitally sign the message, using a certificate. The message can then be sent to any recipient internally or over the Internet.

FIGURE 11.10
The options in the Security tab establish the default encryption for messages.

Many organizations provide certificates to use with GroupWise. Any certificate that supports the Microsoft Cryptography 1.0 API can be used with GroupWise. This includes Novell's Certificate Server. The Help, Help Topics, Index, S/MIME topic contains more information about S/MIME.

NOTE As discussed in Chapter 8, you can set message send options on a message-by-message basis. To set send options for an individual message, open the new message window, click the Send Options tab, click the Security button, and select the appropriate options.

If you click the Advanced Options tab, you will be prompted to configure the default advanced security options.

Advanced Security Options

If you set up security options for encryption and/or digital signatures, you will be prompted for your certificate password for *each* message you send. A portion of your certificate will also be sent with each message for decryption and signature verification.

Your geographic location determines the level of encryption allowed. For example, 128-bit encryption is only allowed in the United States. The

Help, Help Topics, Index, S/MIME topic contains more information about encryption levels.

If you receive a message that has been encrypted or digitally signed, you will be prompted to accept a portion of the certificate. Clicking the Advanced Options button on the Security tab will open up the Advanced Security Options dialog box, shown in Figure 11.11, which enables you to set up the following options:

- ▶ **Encrypted Item**—Establish your preferred encryption algorithm for messages. (The default is 40 bits.)

- ▶ **Signed Item**—Send your message in clear text (default) and/or include your certificate.

- ▶ **Certificate Revocation**—Check incoming signed and encrypted messages for certificates that have been revoked, and set the warning level. (This option is disabled by default.)

- ▶ **S/MIME Compliance Check**—The version of S/MIME that is decided on as the standard for your messages. (Version 3 is the default.)

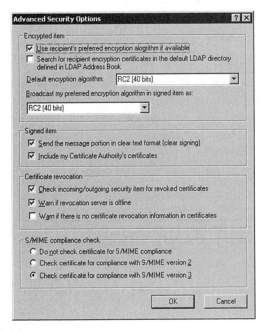

FIGURE 11.11
You use this dialog box to set up the advanced security options, including encryption.

Regardless of whether you access these security options through the Send Options or Security applet, or set them up for each message as you send it, the encryption and digital signatures add a powerful layer of security to the GroupWise messages you send and receive.

Security Options

When you double-click the Security icon, you see the Security Options dialog box. These options affect your entire Mailbox. You can also set up the encryption and digital signature default options using the Send Options tab. Remember, this tab is a duplicate of the Security tab under Send Options.

Password

One of the most important security options is found on the Password tab, which is shown in Figure 11.12. This password is used to enter your Mailbox when GroupWise is started, with the Web access gateway, routed item completion, and Remote Mode configuration.

To set a password on your Mailbox, follow these steps:

1. Double-click the Security icon and click the Password tab once.

2. If you are changing a password, enter your old password in the Old password field.

3. Type a password in the New password field and in the Confirm new password field. Click OK to set the password. The next time you start GroupWise, you must type in your password.

4. Click the Clear Password button if you want to erase your password.

NOTE Keep in mind that your password is case sensitive. Also, even though the administrator can reset it, you should be sure to record your password somewhere secure.

Once you have set up your password, you can move ahead to configuring the Notify options.

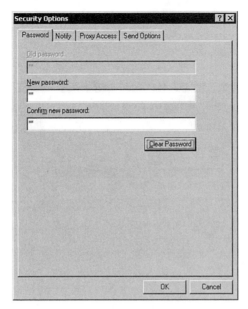

FIGURE 11.12
This dialog box controls the password for your Mailbox.

Notify

The Notify tab enables you to use the Notify program to alert you when you receive a message or when someone else receives a message. You can also be alerted by alarms set in your own Calendar as well as in other peoples' Calendars. As with the Proxy feature, the other person must grant you the right to subscribe to notifications or alarms within his or her Calendar. (See "Proxy" in Chapter 8 for instructions on granting access to your Mailbox.) The Notify tab's options are shown in Figure 11.13.

To receive notification when someone else receives a message (or to be alerted for another person's alarms), follow these steps:

1. Click the Address Book icon to the right of the Name field. Select a user from the list and click OK. Alternatively, you can type the name of the user in the Name field and click Add User.

2. With that person highlighted in the Notification List, check the Subscribe to alarms or Subscribe to notification box. Notice that your name is already on the list.

3. Click OK to apply your change. Your Notify program will now alert you for messages and/or alarms for both yourself and the other users you selected.

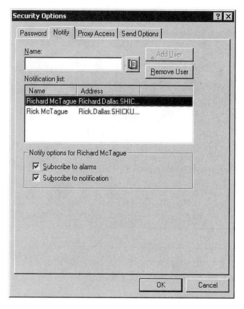

FIGURE 11.13
You can use Notify to be alerted to other user's email messages and appointments.

In the next section, you establish the rights other people have to your Mailbox through Proxy.

Proxy Access

Proxy Access establishes the rights that other users have to your Mailbox when they use Proxy. This is explained in detail in Chapter 8.

Send Options

The Send Options tab of the Security Options dialog box is described in the "Security" section earlier in this chapter.

Certificates

Certificates are used to encrypt, decrypt, digitally sign, and verify messages both internally in your GroupWise system and over the Internet. The Certificates option enables you to set and manage certificates (yours and recipients) for use in GroupWise.

Your public certificate is used to sign messages and to send to others to allow them to verify your signature on the message. Certificates have two elements: a public key and a private key. From the perspective of encrypting and sending a message, once you have imported another user's public certificate, you can encrypt and send messages to that user, using the public key element from the certificate. When the other person receives the encrypted message, that user will use the private key element in his or her certificate to decrypt the message.

From the perspective of receiving an encrypted message, you must have already sent your certificate to the sender. That person will use his or her public key element of your certificate to encrypt the message, and you will use the private key element of your certificate to decrypt the message.

NOTE A further discussion of how to obtain a certificate file and the details of public and private keys is beyond the scope of this book.

My Certificates

The My Certificates dialog box, shown in Figure 11.14, enables you to obtain a certificate, import an existing certificate, or view and manage the properties of your certificate. This dialog box will show a list of your certificates.

You will find the following features on the My Certificates dialog box:

▶ **Get Certificate**—Clicking this button will start your Web browser and point to the Novell GroupWise Certificate page (`www.novell.com/products/groupwise/certified.html`), where you can get information on supported certificates.

▶ **Edit Properties**—This button enables you to edit the properties of your certificate.

FIGURE 11.14
This dialog box is where you configure your certificates to use in encryption.

▶ **Import**—Clicking this button will enable you to browse to the file location of your certificate. Certificate files end with a `.p12` or `.pfx` extension. You will also need to enter your certificate password. The Allow Export of Private Key in the Future option is needed for exporting the private key portion of your certificate to a file for backup or other purposes.

Once you click OK in the Import My Certificate screen, you will be asked to set the security level in the Private Key Container dialog box. Low grants others permission to use your certificate without notification. Medium (the default) requests your permission when the certificate is going to be used, and High requests your permission with your password.

▶ **View Details**—This button enables you to see the detailed information about your certificate.

▶ **Set As Default**—If you have multiple certificates, use this button to designate the default certificate for encrypting and signing messages.

▶ **Certification Path**—This button shows the list of Certificate Authorities (CAs) that provided you with the certificate.

▶ **Export**—This button enables you to export the selected certificate to a file.

▶ **Remove**—This button enables you to remove the selected certificate from use in GroupWise.

These options are needed for most certificate configurations.

Certificate Authorities' Certificates

Clicking the Certificate Authorities' Certificates button brings up a dialog box that displays "Intermediate" and "Root" certificates. These are pre-configured lists of Certificate Authorities used worldwide to enable encryption and digital signatures.

Date Time Options

The Date & Time icon opens the Date Time Options dialog box, shown in Figure 11.15, which contains three option categories: Calendar, Busy Search, and Format.

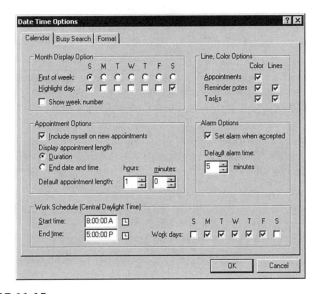

FIGURE 11.15
The Date Time Options dialog box is used to set defaults for Calendar components of GroupWise, such as your work schedule.

Calendar

The Calendar options, shown in Figure 11.15, are described in the following list:

▶ **Month Display Option**—First of week enables you to specify which day you want to display as the first day of the week in your Month Calendar view. Highlight day visually distinguishes the selected days (such as weekends) on the Month Calendar view for quick viewing of the weekdays, for example. Show week number displays the number of the week on the left side of the Month Calendar view.

▶ **Appointment Options**—Include myself on new appointments automatically adds your name as a recipient of any new meeting you create. Display appointment length (Duration) displays the length of time the meeting will take up in hours and minutes. Display appointment length (End date and time) displays the date and time of the meeting. Default Appointment Length specifies the default duration of the appointment messages you send.

▶ **Work Schedule (Time Zone)**—Start time specifies the normal time your workday starts. End time specifies the time your work-day normally ends. Work days specifies your scheduled workdays.

TIP The Work Schedule option will display a different setting when people use Busy Search to invite you to meetings. It also highlights the workdays and times in the Week Calendar view.

▶ **Line, Color Options**—These settings let you customize the appearance of appointments, reminder notes, and tasks in your Calendar with lines and colors.

▶ **Alarm Options**—Use this option to configure whether to set an alarm when an appointment is accepted, and to configure the default alarm interval.

Now that you have configured the main Calendar options, you can set up defaults for using Busy Search.

Busy Search

The Busy Search tab options are shown in Figure 11.16 and discussed in the following list:

▶ **Appointment Length**—Specifies the default length for appointments you create with the Busy Search feature

▶ **Range and Time to Search**—Enables you to specify the default number of days you want to search

▶ **From/To**—Enables you to specify the default time ranges during each day you want searched

▶ **Days to search**—Enables you to choose the default days you want included in the Busy Search

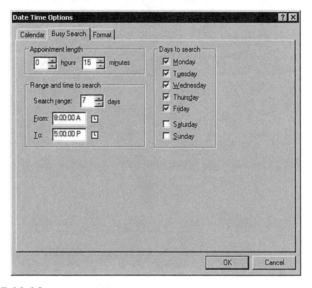

FIGURE 11.16
The Busy Search tab lets you configure the default options for the Busy Search feature.

The Busy Search defaults will be used each time you perform a Busy Search.

Format

The Format tab options enable you to select your preferences for the display of dates and times, as shown in Figure 11.17 and described in the following list:

▶ **System Formats**—Enables you to set the default system time format as well as to access the Windows Regional Settings dialog box

▶ **General GroupWise Format**—Enables you to specify a date and time display format that will be used as the default throughout the GroupWise screens

▶ **Specific GroupWise Formats**—Enables you to specify different formats for the GroupWise main window, properties, and file information

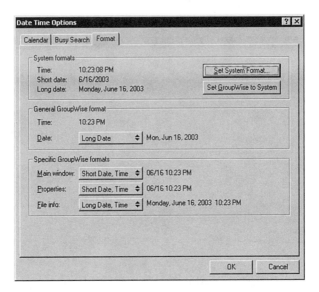

FIGURE 11.17
The Format tab lets you establish the default date and time formats for use by GroupWise.

The default behavior of GroupWise is set up by using the applets described in this section under Tools, Options.

Customizing the Toolbar

You can customize the Toolbar to include the functions and features you use frequently, and you can arrange them in the order that makes the most sense to you.

Toolbars appear in many different GroupWise screens. You have a Toolbar for each message view and for the main GroupWise screen, and you can set different options for each.

To customize any Toolbar, right-click the Toolbar and select Customize Toolbar. The Toolbar Properties dialog box appears, as shown in Figure 11.18.

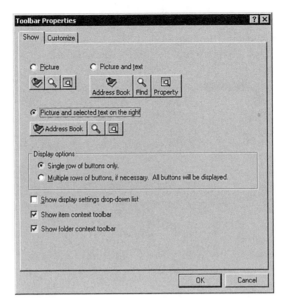

FIGURE 11.18
You can decide to view the buttons on the Toolbar as pictures only or as pictures with text on various rows.

The Show tab enables you to select what should be displayed on the Toolbar—only the picture or both the picture and text. You can also specify one or multiple rows. In addition, you can select whether to display the Display Mode drop-down list in the Toolbar.

The Customize tab, shown in Figure 11.19, enables you to specify which GroupWise features appear on the Toolbar.

Follow these steps to add a menu option to the Toolbar:

1. Click the category the feature belongs to (for example, the Tools category contains options for the Address Book and Hit the Road tools).

2. Double-click the button you want on the Toolbar. The button will appear on the Toolbar.

3. Click and drag the button to your desired location on the Toolbar.

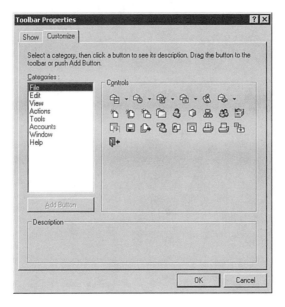

FIGURE 11.19
The Customize tab lets you place the buttons you use most often on the Toolbar for quick, one-click access.

When the Toolbar Properties dialog box is displayed, you can arrange the existing Toolbar buttons by clicking and dragging them to the desired locations. To remove a button from the Toolbar, click the button and drag it off the Toolbar.

Customizing Your Folders

In Chapter 5, "Message Management," you saw how to use folders to help organize your messages. By adjusting the properties of the folders in your Mailbox, you can arrange to see folder contents when a folder is opened, see who has access to the messages in the folder (if anyone), and specify what columns are displayed. Each folder can be customized individually. For example, the Mailbox can be set up to display only the Subject and From fields, and the Sent Items folder can be set up to display Subject, Opened Status, and Date fields.

Property Sets

Even though you can set up a parent/child folder structure, folder properties are set for each folder individually. These folder properties are grouped into the following sets:

- ▶ **General**—Holds general information about the folder, such as the owner and a description

- ▶ **Display**—Configures folder settings to determine how messages are displayed in the folder and what columns are used

- ▶ **Sharing**—Determines access to the messages in the folder

---

NOTE The people who share a particular parent folder will not necessarily share the subfolders under the folder. Shared access to folders is set for the individual folder.

The properties available for folders differ, depending on the type of folder you are configuring. All folders contain the General and Display tabs. The Trash folder contains a Cleanup property tab.

TIP When you right-click the Cabinet, you can select Sort Subfolders to quickly alphabetize the first-level subfolders. To sort a set of nested folders, you need to select Sort Subfolders from the parent folder.

User-created folders contain a unique tab called *Sharing*. The Sharing tab enables you to share the folders with other GroupWise users.

To display or change the properties of a folder, simply right-click the folder and choose Properties.

General

The general folder properties are shown in Figure 11.20 and described in the following list:

- ▶ **Type**—Describes the type of folder: Personal, Calendar, Mailbox, and so on

- ▶ **Owner**—Specifies the creator of the folder

- ▶ **Contains**—Provides a summary of the folder's contents

- ▶ **Description**—Gives a general description of the folder

Once you configure the general options for a folder, you can customize the display settings.

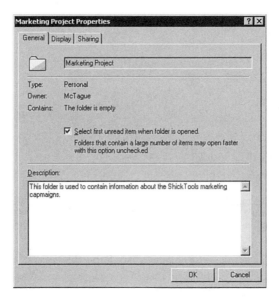

FIGURE 11.20
The General tab contains the name, owner, and other information about the folder.

Display

Figure 11.21 depicts the Display tab of a personal folder. This setting configures the default display options. The Display drop-down list on the Toolbar enables you to configure momentary display options, not default display properties. Every time the folder is accessed, the settings you make in the Display tab of the folder properties will be active.

NOTE If you would like to save a custom set of folder settings, click the Save As button, enter a name for the folder setting, and click OK. Your new custom set will appear under the Setting name drop-down list.

Here's a list of the settings you'll find in the Display tab:

▶ **Setting Name**—A drop-down list of preconfigured folder settings.

▶ **Description**—A description of this group of folder settings.

▶ **View By**—Sets the display to the Message Details, Message Thread, or Calendar format for the items in this folder.

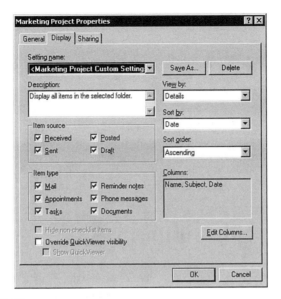

FIGURE 11.21
The Display tab allows you to customize the viewing and sorting options for
the folder.

- ▶ **Sort By**—Determines a piece of information about the messages by
  which all messages in this folder will be sorted (for example, Date,
  From, and so on).

- ▶ **Sort Order**—Specifies an ascending or descending display of the
  items in this folder.

- ▶ **Item Source**—Tells GroupWise what the originating source is of
  the messages in this folder: Received, Sent, Posted, or Draft.

- ▶ **Item Type**—Specifies the types of messages contained in the folder: Mail, Appointments, Reminder notes, Tasks, Documents, and
  Phone Messages.

- ▶ **Columns**—Determines which pieces of information will appear in
  the columns in the Items Area. (Choose Edit Columns to add or
  delete columns.)

TIP Make sure the piece of information by which you are sorting the messages is also a column.

Once you have set up the display options, you can establish shared folders.

Sharing

Sharing options for folders determine who has access to the messages inside of them. Chapter 5 discusses how to use shared folders in detail.

These settings allowed you to customize your folders. The next section describes another customization feature: Show Appointment As.

Show Appointment As

The Show Appointment As option lets you specify an appointment with different "busy properties." For example, when you create a new appointment, you can set it up as a "tentative" appointment that can be scheduled over, or you can set up a period of time (an appointment) as time "out of the office." People who perform a Busy Search will see the different types of appointments and have more information about your schedule than just "busy."

Free, Tentative, Busy, and Out Of Office are the four options to choose from to assign to an existing appointment in the Calendar. To set this option, highlight the appointment, choose Show Appointment As from the Actions menu, and select one of the four choices, as shown in Figure 11.22.

TIP Right-clicking an appointment brings up a QuickMenu with the Show Appointment As option available.

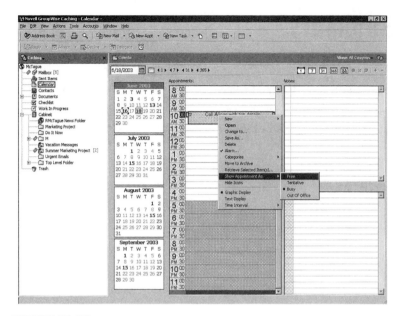

FIGURE 11.22
You can show your appointments as Free, Tentative, Busy, or Out Of Office with this option.

Headers

You can change the look and feel of the headers in GroupWise (the area between the Toolbars and the messages and Calendar information).

By placing your mouse pointer in a header area and clicking the right mouse button, you can change the header color, text color, and font size. This makes GroupWise much more readable and provides more contrasts with different colors.

If you make a change to the header that you don't want anymore, you can choose Reset to Defaults on the QuickMenu, accessed with the right mouse button.

Summary

In this chapter, we discussed the capabilities for customizing your GroupWise program—from setting your GroupWise defaults, to customizing the look, feel, and content of Toolbars, headers, and folders.

You saw specific examples, and we covered every possible customization capability in GroupWise to allow you to configure the program to your unique tastes.

In Chapter 12, "Mobile GroupWise Access," we will look into accessing GroupWise on a personal digital assistant (PDA).

CHAPTER 12

Mobile GroupWise Access

One of the best features of GroupWise is its ability to provide access to your information—anywhere, anytime. For example, you could be visiting relatives and need to check your Address Book for a phone number. You can simply start a Web browser, open the GroupWise WebAccess client, and look in your address books for the number you need.

With the advent of wireless personal digital assistants (PDAs), this need for mobile access to GroupWise has greatly increased. Novell has met this need by building into the GroupWise system the ability to access your GroupWise information from any PDA that can access the Internet.

We will explore both the WebAccess and wireless client experiences in this chapter, starting with WebAccess.

Using GroupWise WebAccess

The WebAccess version of the GroupWise client enables you to access your GroupWise Mailbox from your Web browser, no matter where you happen to be in the world. With WebAccess, you can check your messages or send new GroupWise messages, process incoming messages, check your Calendar, schedule appointments, send tasks, and more. You can use WebAccess to do almost all the GroupWise tasks you would do from the regular GroupWise client.

GroupWise 6.5 WebAccess comes in two versions: the Java-enhanced version and the "non-Java" version. If your machine has the power and your browser supports Java, you should use the Java version. For under-powered machines or nonstandard browsers, use the non-Java version. The figures in this chapter show the Java-enabled version.

NOTE The GroupWise system must be properly configured before you can access your Mailbox from your Web browser. Ask your system administrator if your GroupWise system supports WebAccess.

The concepts behind the topics discussed in this chapter (for example, when a task should be used in the Calendar instead of an appointment) won't be covered here; you can refer to earlier chapters for additional background information. We will focus on how you perform these tasks in the WebAccess client in this chapter.

Some functions are available in the 32-bit client program that you can't access using GroupWise WebAccess, such as setting up personal Calendar items, discussion thread views, saving draft messages, filters, POP3/IMAP/NNTP access, multiple Calendar print options, sharing address books, creating and managing shared folders (although you can see the information in them), and resending items.

GroupWise 6.5 WebAccess has four major new features:

▶ The ability to "proxy" other's Mailboxes

▶ The ability to configure sending options, such as the priority

▶ The Find function

▶ Additional Mailbox-configuration options, such as vacation rules

We will cover all these features in this chapter.

Even if those features weren't available, you would still find the GroupWise WebAccess client to be a powerful, quick, and easy-to-use interface into your GroupWise information.

Running WebAccess

To run the WebAccess GroupWise client, simply launch your Web browser and go to the URL established for WebAccess. The correct URL depends on how your administrator has set up the system. Ask your administrator for the URL you should use. When you access your WebAccess address, you will encounter the login screen shown in Figure 12.1.

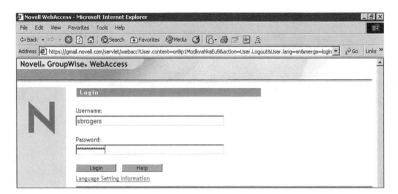

FIGURE 12.1
The WebAccess login page will prompt you for your Mailbox ID and password.

Enter your GroupWise user ID and your Mailbox password (which is required) and click the Login button. The WebAccess main screen, shown in Figure 12.2, appears automatically. You can access all the messaging features of GroupWise from the main screen.

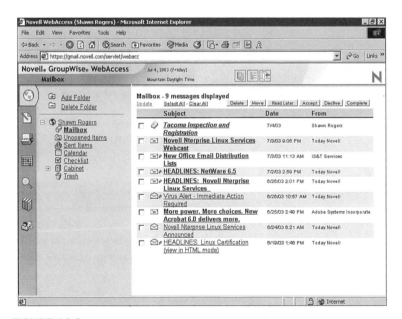

FIGURE 12.2
The WebAccess main screen gives you one-click access to most functions you will need.

The GroupWise WebAccess client functions like a regular Web page. To read a mail message, simply click your mouse on the message in your Mailbox. A typical mail message is shown in Figure 12.3.

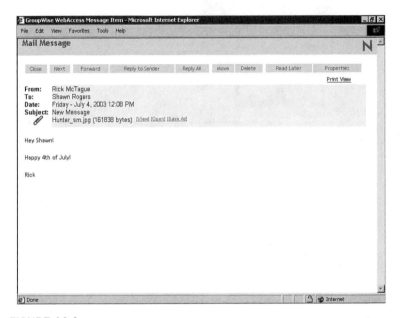

FIGURE 12.3
This screen shows a typical email message with a file attachment.

Notice that the typical mail message actions are available on the Toolbar, located just above the message. Attachments are shown listed with the message, and you can either view them or save the files to another location.

Because using the GroupWise WebAccess client is very intuitive if you've used the regular GroupWise client (and have read this book), we won't kill any more trees to document all the messaging features. We'll just show you how to send an email message to help you get oriented, and then we'll show you some of the few features that are significantly different from the regular GroupWise client.

Sending Messages

Sending messages from the WebAccess client is as simple as reading them. The Compose button on the left side of the main WebAccess screen allows you to create a new message. A new WebAccess mail message screen is shown in Figure 12.4. Enter each field just as you would normally and click Send when you're done.

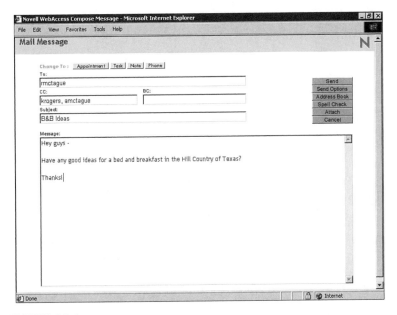

FIGURE 12.4
You can send messages easily with WebAccess using this screen.

> **TIP** Use the Change To buttons at the top of the screen to create appointments, notes, tasks, or phone messages.

To attach a file, click the Attach button and use the Browse button to find the files to attach. Click Add to add the files to the attachment list, and click OK when you're done. The Send Options button allows you to set the classification, priority, reply options, and return notification on the message, and the Spell Check button will launch a spell checker for this message.

> **NOTE** Because the WebAccess client doesn't distinguish between "personal" and "group" Calendar items, you can send an appointment to yourself to place it on your Calendar. This has the same effect as a personal Calendar item.

Managing Messages

From the main screen, you can click the check box next to any message (or multiple messages) and use the following buttons to manage it:

- ▶ **Delete**—Deletes the message from the Mailbox
- ▶ **Move**—Moves the message to a folder
- ▶ **Read Later**—Marks the message as unopened
- ▶ **Accept**—Accepts the appointment, task, or reminder note
- ▶ **Decline**—Declines the appointment, task, or reminder note
- ▶ **Complete**—Completes the task

With these buttons, you can manage your messages using the WebAccess client.

Managing the Address Book

The WebAccess Address Book interface is a bit different from that of the regular GroupWise client. You have a choice between using the Java, HTML, or LDAP version of the Address Book. The HTML version is shown in Figure 12.5; the Java version is used throughout the rest of this chapter. If your system administrator has configured an LDAP Address Book, you can use the WebAccess client to display the entries in it. To open the Address Book, click the card file button on the left side of the main screen.

To find names in the Address Book while you are composing a new message, click the Address Book button at the right of the new mail message you are writing.

To view all names in the Address Book, leave the name fields empty and click the Search button (Search Address Book in the Java version). By default, the Address Book displays only 25 names at a time, so using this method could get tedious because you have to wait for the results of each address lookup to load from the Web server.

TIP You can specify that more names appear after each search by clicking the Number of names to display drop-down box and choosing a higher value. However, this will increase the time it takes to download the results of each search.

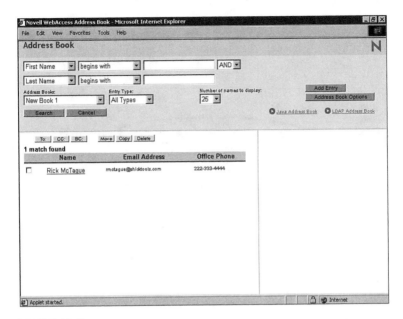

FIGURE 12.5
The HTML version of the GroupWise WebAccess Address Book provides
access to all your personal address books.

To narrow your search, use the asterisk (*) wildcard, such as entering J*
in the First Name field and **Do*** in the Last Name field to find all people
with first names beginning with J and last names beginning with Do.
When you locate the name you want, click the To, CC, or BC button to
enter the name and then click OK to close. The message will be
addressed to the recipients you chose.

You can use the WebAccess client to create, delete, and modify entries in
any of your personal or shared address books.

Managing the Address Book Entries
From the main screen of the Address Book, you can manage the entries
in the selected book using the buttons in the middle of the screen shown
in Figure 12.6.

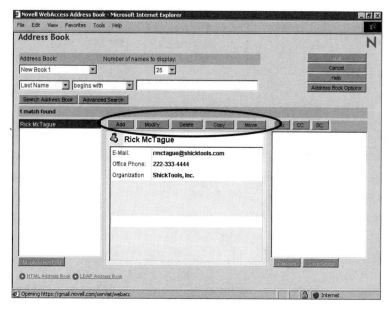

FIGURE 12.6
The buttons in the middle portion of the Address Book allow you to manage the entries.

The Address Book buttons are explained in the following list:

- ▶ **Add**—Opens a new screen to create a new entry in the selected address book, as shown in Figure 12.7

- ▶ **Modify**—Allows you to change the information about a contact in an address book

- ▶ **Delete**—Deletes the selected Address Book entry

- ▶ **Copy**—Copies the selected Address Book entry from one book to another

- ▶ **Move**—Moves the selected Address Book entry from one book to another

Using these features lets you manage the contacts in your address books.

Managing the Address Books
Click the Address Book Options button and you will see the screen shown in Figure 12.8. You use this screen to manage the Address Book itself (not the entries).

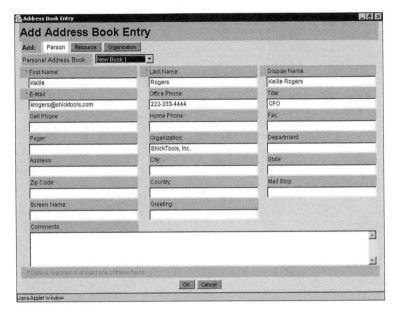

FIGURE 12.7
Adding a contact provides many fields for a new Address Book entry.

Select the Personal Address Books entry from the list and then choose
from the following options:

- ▶ **Create Address Book**—Use this button to create additional personal address books.

- ▶ **Delete**—Use this button to delete the selected personal address book.

- ▶ **Modify**—Use this button to rename or change the description of the selected personal address book.

- ▶ **Save As**—Use this button to copy the selected personal address book to another, new address book.

These options let you manage (modify and other tasks) an entire personal
address book at a time.

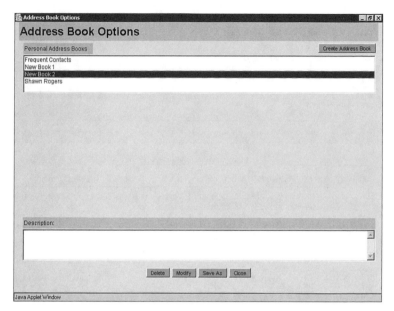

FIGURE 12.8
This screen lets you manage the Address Book.

Using the Calendar

You can manage your Calendar using the WebAccess client, much in the same way the regular 32-bit client is used. Accessing and creating appointments, reminder notes, and tasks are very easy using the WebAccess client.

As with the Address Book, there are two "flavors" of the Calendar: HTML and Java. We will focus on the Java version in this section. Clicking the View Calendar button (the fourth button on the left of the main screen) will display your Calendar entries, as shown in Figure 12.9.

Use the Appointments, Notes, and Tasks buttons to add or remove these items from the display. You can also navigate to the desired date by clicking the left/right arrows or by using the Go To Date window, shown in Figure 12.10, which is accessed by clicking the Go To Date button.

Click the date (if you're in the current month) or use the single (monthly) or double (yearly) navigation buttons and then click OK. The Calendar information for that date will be displayed.

Clicking the Launch Month Calendar button displays a month-at-a-glance view of your Calendar, as shown in Figure 12.11.

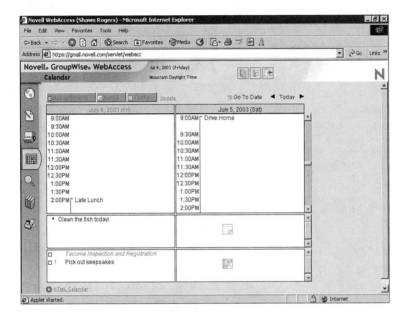

FIGURE 12.9
The WebAccess GroupWise Calendar lets you manage your appointments, notes, and tasks.

Use the Month buttons at the bottom of the screen to navigate to a different month, or use the left/right arrows at the lower-right corner of the screen to move to a different month.

TIP To see the details about a specific Calendar event, just place your mouse over the event and a "bubble" window will appear with the details listed. You can also double-click an entry, which will open a new browser window with all the details listed.

Accessing Other Mailboxes (Proxy)

One of the more powerful new features of the GroupWise WebAccess client is the ability to access other mailboxes—the Proxy feature.

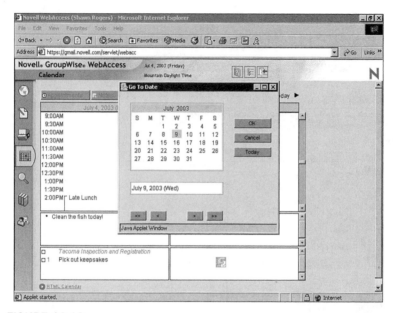

FIGURE 12.10
The Go To Date window provides an easy way to navigate to a particular date.

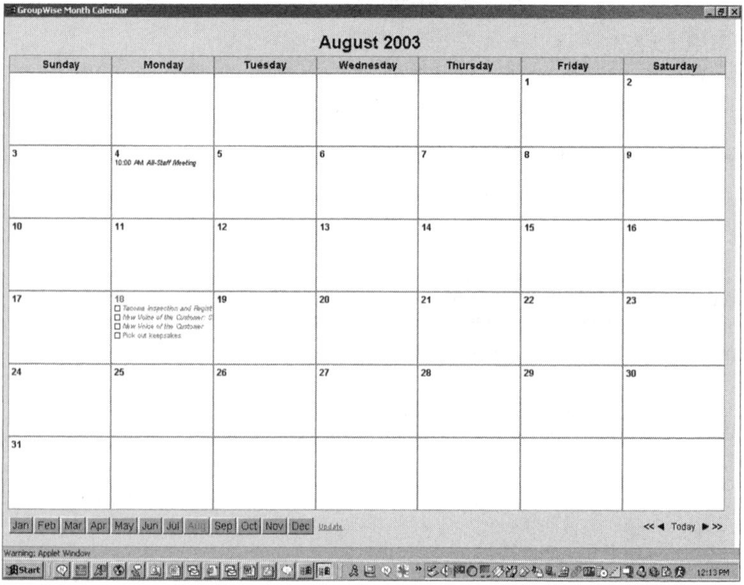

FIGURE 12.11
This screen shows the monthly view of the Calendar.

> **NOTE** Remember, each user controls the security on his or her Mailbox. You have to be granted permission to access another Mailbox. This can be done with the WebAccess client, as described later in this chapter, or with the 32-bit client, as described in Chapter 8, "Advanced Features."

To start a Proxy session, click the seventh icon on the left side of the main screen, the Proxy button. You will then see the screen shown in Figure 12.12.

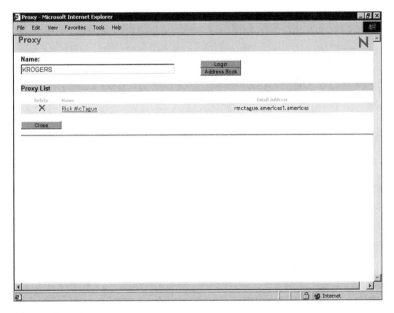

FIGURE 12.12
You can access other Mailboxes using the GroupWise WebAccess Proxy screen.

Enter the Mailbox name (if known) or use the Address Book button to browse the system address book to find the Mailbox name. Then click Login. You will now see the main WebAccess screen, but the information will be from the other user's Mailbox (not your own). You will be able to perform the actions (read, write, and so on) that the user has granted you. Chapter 8 discusses Proxy in more detail. To end the Proxy session, simply close the screen. The next time you want to proxy that user, he or she will be listed in the Proxy screen, as shown in Figure 12.12.

Using GroupWise WebAccess Find

The GroupWise 6.5 WebAccess client adds the powerful Find utility to allow quick location of messages that meet certain criteria. You won't be able to build a complex search (as discussed in Chapter 5, "Message Management"), but you can search using many common criteria. The magnifying glass button on the left side of the main GroupWise WebAccess screen will open the Find screen, shown in Figure 12.13.

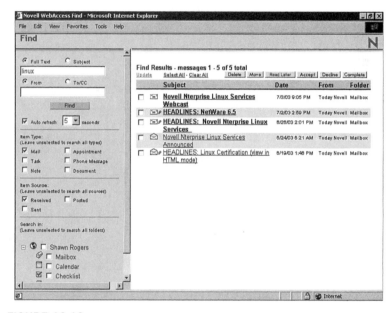

FIGURE 12.13
The GroupWise WebAccess Find utility is an excellent tool for searching and locating messages with specific content.

To use Find, simply click your selections, enter in the text you want to search for (if desired), select the folders to search (leave them all unselected for a full Mailbox search), and click the Find button. The results will be displayed on the right side of the screen.

Configuring Mailbox Options

As discussed in Chapter 11, "Customizing GroupWise," you have many options for customizing your Mailbox, such as the signature, default send options, password, and so on. The GroupWise WebAccess client gives you access to the more commonly used options. Click the Options button (the middle button in the group of three buttons along the top of the main WebAccess screen), and the screen shown in Figure 12.14 will be displayed.

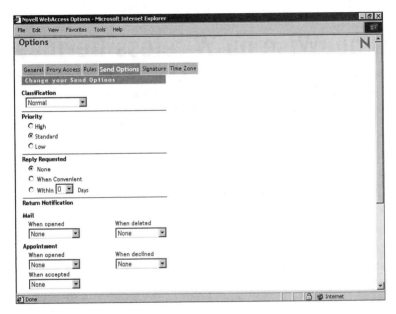

FIGURE 12.14
You can configure your Mailbox options from the GroupWise WebAccess client using this screen (Send Options shown).

The following tabs are available in the Mailbox Options screen:

▶ **General**—Used to configure the number of messages displayed in one screen.

▶ **Proxy Access**—Used to grant or modify rights to others for accessing your Mailbox.

▶ **Rules**—Used to set up basic rules (Delete, Forward, Move to Folder, Reply, Vacation).

▶ **Send Options**—Includes default classification, priority, reply, and notification options.

▶ **Signature**—Used to provide the text to be added at the end of sent messages.

▶ **Time Zone**—Used to configure your local time zone. This applies only to the GroupWise WebAccess account, not to your master Mailbox.

Make your selections and click Save to apply them to your Mailbox.

GroupWise on Wireless Devices

The proliferation of wireless handheld devices has brought the power of the Internet to the palm of your hand. GroupWise has taken advantage of this handheld mobility by providing a WebAccess interface that lets you manage your GroupWise Mailbox and perform many of the most common GroupWise tasks from the convenience and portability of your handheld device.

This part of the chapter provides an overview of how to access your GroupWise Mailbox and perform basic messaging tasks using your personal digital assistant (PDA) and the special PDA version of WebAccess.

It is important that you understand the difference between *accessing* and *synchronizing* when talking about PDAs. GroupWise allows you *access*, meaning that if your PDA can open a Web browser and see Web pages, it can access your GroupWise information.

Synchronizing is a software-based means to copy the information in your GroupWise Mailbox to your PDA, where you can access it regardless of whether you are connected to the Internet. This is accomplished with third-party software tools. You can see some of those tools for many PDAs at www.novell.com/products/groupwise/partners/#pda.

System Requirements

Before you can use your handheld device to access GroupWise, the following requirements must be met:

▶ Your GroupWise system administrator must have configured the GroupWise system to support PDA WebAccess.

▶ You must have a PDA, wireless phone, or other handheld device that supports the Wireless Access Protocol (WAP). The device must have a microbrowser that uses Handheld Device Markup Language

(HDML) 3.0 (or above) or Wireless Markup Language (WML) 1.1 (or above). The device must have wireless access to the Internet (or it must be able to access the Internet through a host PC to which the device can be connected). If you have a Palm OS device, you must be running a version of the Palm OS that supports Web Clipping Applications (PQAs). All versions of the Windows CE or Microsoft Pocket PC OS are supported.

▶ You must have an account on the GroupWise system with a password set on your Mailbox.

NOTE This chapter was written using a Compaq iPAQ model 3975 running Microsoft Pocket PC Version 3.0 and Microsoft Pocket Internet Explorer. Internet access was achieved using an expansion sleeve and a wireless LAN card linking to a wireless access point. Screen captures were created using the Microsoft Remote Display utility. Please note that the drop-down menu options shown in the graphics in this chapter are menu options for the Remote Control Utility and not menu options for GroupWise PDA WebAccess. Those menu options will not appear on the screen of your wireless device.

Accessing Your GroupWise Mailbox

To access your GroupWise Mailbox with your handheld device, follow these steps:

1. Validate that you have a wireless connection, and run the Web browser on your device.

2. Enter the address (URL) to the PDA WebAccess page. Your system administrator must provide this address to you. The GroupWise login screen displays, as shown in Figure 12.15.

3. Enter your GroupWise user ID and your Mailbox password and then tap Login. The main GroupWise screen displays, as shown in Figure 12.16.

The main GroupWise screen lets you access the major GroupWise features. The features corresponding to each of the icons shown in Figure 12.16 are described in the following subsections.

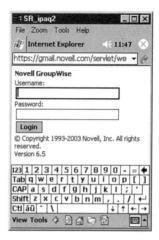

FIGURE 12.15
The login screen requests your login ID and GroupWise password.

FIGURE 12.16
This PDA WebAccess screen provides access to the most common GroupWise functions.

TIP Every screen that you access from this main screen has a link at the top labeled Main Menu. This link will always return you to the main GroupWise screen shown in Figure 12.16.

Mailbox

Tap the Mailbox link to open your GroupWise Mailbox, as shown in Figure 12.17.

FIGURE 12.17
The PDA WebAccess Mailbox lets you manage your GroupWise messages.

Notice that the Mailbox is very similar in appearance to the typical WebAccess Mailbox, as explained previously in this chapter. You can open any message simply by tapping the subject line. You can perform other operations by tapping in the check box and then tapping on the button at the top of the screen.

NOTE If you use the Change Folder option to access a folder other than your Mailbox folder and then you later return to the main menu, the last folder you accessed will be listed on the main screen, instead of the main Mailbox folder. If you use the Back button on your browser, the main Mailbox folder will still display.

Folders

The Folders link takes you to a view of your GroupWise system folders and also your Cabinet, as shown in Figure 12.18.

You can expand and collapse the Folders view by tapping the plus or minus icon or the up or down arrow (depending on your WebAccess configuration). To access the items in a folder, simply tap that folder.

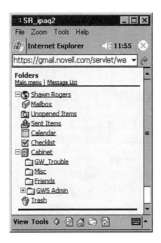

FIGURE 12.18
Tap the Folders link to view your GroupWise system and Cabinet folders.

When you are viewing the contents of a folder, you can return to the folder display by tapping the Change Folder link at the top of the screen.

Calendar

The Calendar link takes you to the Calendar view for the current day and displays the day's appointments, notes, and tasks, as shown in Figure 12.19.

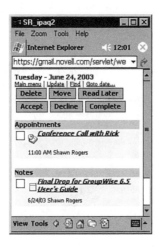

FIGURE 12.19
The Calendar view shows the current day's appointments, notes, and tasks.

Click the Goto date link to access the appointments, notes, and tasks for a different date.

Find

The Find option is a very useful tool for the wireless WebAccess client. It allows you to quickly locate information contained in your GroupWise Mailbox based on text in the Subject line, names in the From line, the item type, the item source (received, posted, or sent), and the folder or folders in which the item might be located.

Compose

The Compose button lets you create GroupWise messages. When you tap Compose, you see the screen shown in Figure 12.20.

FIGURE 12.20
The Compose link lets you create GroupWise appointments, tasks, notes, and phone messages.

By default, you will be creating a mail message when you tap Compose. Tap a different item type button to compose a different GroupWise message type.

You can tap the Address Book to locate the message recipients. Tap any of the text fields to input the subject and message using your handheld device's preferred text-entry method.

Tap the Send button to send the message.

Address Book

The Address Book option brings up a search screen that lets you search for individuals in the GroupWise or LDAP Address Book, as shown in Figure 12.21. You can enter a first name and/or a last name (the asterisk is acceptable as a wildcard character). You can select the Search option or scroll down and specify how many names to display in the results.

FIGURE 12.21
The Address Book lets you search the GroupWise or LDAP Address Book.

You can tap the down arrow in the Address Books field and select any of your personal address books you have configured. When a personal address book (such as Frequent Contacts) is active, you can tap the Add Entry icon at the bottom of the screen to add contacts to the personal address book.

Documents

The Documents option on the main menu brings up the Document Search function, which lets you search for documents in all available document libraries, as shown in Figure 12.22.

You can search in all document fields by selecting the Anywhere option, or you can search by subject or author. All available document libraries are displayed by scrolling down the screen. Place a check mark in the box next to any library that might contain the document you want to locate.

FIGURE 12.22
Use the Document Search option to find documents in GroupWise document libraries.

Options

The Options link allows you to set a new GroupWise password on your Mailbox by entering your old password, entering a new password, and then confirming your new password.

Exit

The Exit button on the main GroupWise screen terminates your GroupWise session and returns you to the main GroupWise WebAccess login screen.

Summary

In this chapter, we discussed the two major ways you can access GroupWise while you are mobile, whether you are traveling, are on an Internet kiosk, have Internet access using a Web browser, or have a mobile handheld device. This chapter walked you through the process of using GroupWise on both a Web browser and a handheld device, such as a PDA or telephone with wireless Web access capabilities. The WebAccess client gives you access to all your GroupWise information from a Web browser.

GroupWise Startup Options

The GroupWise Startup screen, shown in Figure A.1, is an introductory screen you might see when you run the GroupWise client software. You often will see the Startup screen when you run the GroupWise program for the first time after installation.

FIGURE A.1
The GroupWise Startup screen prompts for critical startup information.

The GroupWise Startup screen will display if, for some reason, the GroupWise system does not recognize your network login ID or your GroupWise user ID. In this situation, you will be prompted to enter the startup information. The GroupWise system requires this information in order to locate your master mailbox on the network.

If the Startup screen displays, the first item to check is your GroupWise user ID and password. If the correct ID does not display, type it in and choose OK.

If your user ID is correct, you need to provide GroupWise with instructions for connecting to your mailbox.

Helping GroupWise Locate Your Mailbox

Depending on your system's configuration, you will need to provide the GroupWise client with one of the following pieces of information:

- ▶ TCP/IP address and port
- ▶ The path to your caching mailbox
- ▶ The path to your remote mailbox

Entering Online Information

To access your master mailbox, you will need to provide your username and password and a valid TCP/IP address and port in the Online Address and Port fields.

The Online Address field requires the IP address of the post office agent. This is *not* the IP address of your workstation. The Port field requires an IP port number. Again, you need to ask your system administrator for the information to be entered. You could also ask another GroupWise user to check the Help, About GroupWise screen and tell you the IP address that displays in the dialog box (the default GroupWise port number is 1677, but that can be configured differently by the GroupWise administrator).

Entering Caching Information

If you are using GroupWise in the Caching Mode (explained in Chapter 10, "Remote Access"), you will need to enter a local path to your GroupWise cache directory. You might need to open Windows Explorer to discover this path, or you can ask your administrator. A sample path is shown earlier in Figure A.1.

Entering Remote Information

If you are starting GroupWise in the Remote Mode (explained in Chapter 10), you will need to enter a local path to your GroupWise remote directory. You might need to open Windows Explorer to discover this path, or you can ask your administrator. A sample path is shown earlier in Figure A.1.

Connecting to GroupWise

After you enable GroupWise to locate your messages by following the preceding instructions, you should be able to click OK to log on to your GroupWise system. When you click OK, you will see a message indicating that you are connecting to GroupWise.

If GroupWise still cannot find your mailbox after you enter an IP address and port (this usually occurs as a result of a system failure), it runs in Remote Mode or Caching Mode. You will still be able to use GroupWise offline and will be able to send and receive messages when the system comes back online.

Calling Up the Startup Dialog Box

You can instruct GroupWise to display the GroupWise Startup screen every time it launches by simply adding a few characters to the GroupWise startup properties. Startup properties are parameters stored along with the GroupWise icon (depending on the version of Windows you are using) that tell GroupWise what to do when it launches. Often, it is necessary to bring up the Startup screen when multiple users run GroupWise from the same computer.

To bring up the GroupWise Startup screen upon launching, follow these steps:

1. Right-click the GroupWise icon and select Properties from the menu.

2. Click the Shortcut tab.

3. Place the cursor in the Target field and go to the end of the command line.

4. Add a space, followed by /@u-?, after the **GRPWISE.EXE** command. Be sure to include a space between the command line and the /

character. Figure A.2 shows the Properties screen with an example of the correct parameter syntax.

5. Select OK. The next time you double-click the GroupWise icon, you will see the GroupWise Startup screen.

FIGURE A.2
Use this syntax to force GroupWise to launch with the Startup screen displayed.

If you want to create multiple GroupWise icons, one for each person who uses the computer, follow the same steps listed previously, but substitute each user's GroupWise ID in place of the question mark in step 4. This permits several users to run GroupWise from a single machine; however, all users will share the same GroupWise default settings.

NOTE All users who run GroupWise from a shared computer should set passwords on their GroupWise mailboxes. This prevents the users from accessing each others' mailboxes.

To allow multiple users on the same machine to have different default settings in GroupWise, you must enable multiple user logins for Windows by creating multiple user profiles. Refer to your Windows documentation for instructions.

Other Useful GroupWise Startup Options

In addition to the /@u-? startup option described previously, you can use several other startup options to alter the behavior of GroupWise 6.5. Table A.1 describes several of these useful GroupWise startup options, and a complete list of startup switches can be found in the GroupWise documentation located on the Novell Web site at www.novell.com/ documentation/lg/gw65/index.html under the heading "Using Startup Options."

TABLE A.1   Useful GroupWise Startup Switches

SYNTAX	FUNCTION
/@u-userID	Allows you to launch GroupWise and access your mailbox from another user's computer while the other user is still logged on to the network.
/bl	Launches GroupWise without displaying the GroupWise splash screen (but does not actually speed up the loading of the program).
/c	Causes GroupWise to check for unopened items. If unopened items exist in your mailbox, GroupWise opens as usual. If no unopened items are found, GroupWise does not load.
/iabs	Causes the Address Book application to load. This results in a slightly slower GroupWise launch time but causes the Address Book to open much quicker when you access it for the first time in GroupWise.

You can string multiple GroupWise startup switches together on the program line simply by placing a space between the startup switches.

GroupWise Resources

If you have read the entire *Novell GroupWise 6.5 User's Handbook* and are still uncertain as to how to perform a function in GroupWise, check the index at the back of the book for topics you might have missed. If you still can't find the answer, you should investigate the GroupWise Online Help system. This appendix explains how to use the Online Help resources available for GroupWise.

Using the F1 Key

The F1 (Help) key provides immediate context-sensitive help for most screens in the GroupWise client program. Simply press F1 at any time in GroupWise for assistance with your current task.

Using the Help Button

In most GroupWise dialog boxes, a Help button is available for quick assistance with the options in the dialog box. Click this button to view an in-depth explanation of the dialog box or feature you're using. The help information typically explains options and provides examples of how to use the dialog box.

About Toolbar Help

If you allow the mouse pointer to rest for more than a second or two over any Toolbar button, a pop-up window displays, telling you what function that button performs.

Using the Help Menu

The Help menu offers different options depending on the features of GroupWise with which you are working. For example, in the main GroupWise screen, the Help menu topics cover general GroupWise features. In the Address Book, the Help menu topics relate to using the Address Book.

From the main GroupWise screen, the Help, Help Topics option opens the screen shown in Figure B.1.

FIGURE B.1
The GroupWise Help screen provides detailed assistance on GroupWise features.

With the Contents tab selected, you can navigate to your desired topic by expanding the headings in the left pane and then highlighting the specific topic you want to view.

With the Index tab selected, you can type the first few letters of the topic you want to view, and the list will automatically scroll to that topic.

With the Search tab selected, you can enter a search string and click the List Topics button to see topics related to your search criteria.

When you have located the topic you want to learn about, double-click that topic or click the Display button.

Viewing the Online GroupWise User's Guide

Click Help, User's Guide to access the GroupWise documentation from the Novell Web site. You can view the documentation in HTML format, or you can download the PDF file to view with Adobe Acrobat Reader.

You can also access the GroupWise User's Guide by pointing your Web browser to the following URL:

`http://www.novell.com/documentation/lg/gw65/index.html`

Information About GroupWise Cool Solutions

The Cool Solutions option launches your Web browser and takes you to the Novell GroupWise magazine Web site at `www.novell.com/coolsolutions/gwmag/index.html`.

GroupWise Cool Solutions is an online GroupWise magazine that is updated frequently with the latest tips and tricks for using GroupWise.

Accessing the Novell GroupWise Product Information Page

You can access general information about the entire GroupWise product, including the GroupWise clients and the GroupWise administration system, by clicking Help, Novell GroupWise Home Page or by pointing your Web browser to `www.novell.com/products/groupwise`.

Tip of the Day

When you click Help, Tip of the Day, you see the screen shown in Figure B.2.

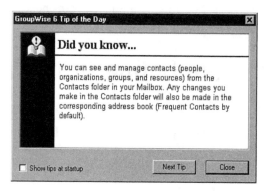

FIGURE B.2
The Tip of the Day feature lets you improve your GroupWise skills one day at a time.

This feature presents a Tip of the Day every time you launch GroupWise if you select the Show tips at startup option at the bottom of the dialog box.

About GroupWise

The Help, About GroupWise screen, shown in Figure B.3, is useful when you are troubleshooting problems with GroupWise.

The Program Release line shows you the exact version and release date of the GroupWise client you are running, as well as the location from which you are running the client (such as your local hard drive or a network location).

The Username line shows your GroupWise user ID and your GroupWise file ID. (The file ID is used to identify which files in the GroupWise post office message repository relate to your GroupWise mailbox. This is useful for support personnel working on GroupWise system-level problems.)

FIGURE B.3
The About GroupWise screen provides useful system information.

The Post Office line specifies in which post office your GroupWise mailbox is located. Depending on your system configuration, many post offices are likely configured for your organization.

The Path to Post Office line provides a path to the post office (if you are connected directly by a drive mapping), or it shows the IP address and the IP port you are using to connect to your post office.

INDEX

multi-user Calendar

managing, 141

users, adding, 141

Multi-User List dialog box, 141

Multi-User view (Calendar), 114-116

multiple windows, opening (Proxy), 158

My Certificates dialog box, 263

Certification Path option, 264

Edit Properties option, 263

Export option, 264

Get Certificate option, 263

Import option, 264

Remove option, 264

View Details option, 264

My Subject feature, 23, 165

N - O

Name Completion address feature, 37

navigating main GroupWise screen, 11

keystroke shortcuts, 12

QuickMenus, 12

QuickViewer, 12

Toolbar, 11

networks, Remote Mode connections, 226, 233-234

New Book command (file menu), 60

New Contacts dialog box, 23

New Document dialog box, 204-206

new features

functionality

Address Book enhancements, 23

Address Selector, 23

From feature, 23

iCal Internet appointments, 25

junk mail handling, 25

message categories, 22

My Subject feature, 23

security enhancements, 24

look and feel, 15

Calendar enhancements, 19-20

filter enhancements, 19

headers, 16-17

mode selection, 17

read views, 16

Toolbar enhancements, 21

management

Checklist folder, 26

Contacts folder, 26

Tabbed Item Views, 26

New Mail button (Toolbar), 11, 38

New Main Window command (Window menu), 158

New menu commands

Appointment, 33, 126

Folder, 73

Mail, 11, 38

Phone Message, 35

Reminder Note, 34, 132

Task, 34, 131

New Rule dialog box, 148

New Task button (Toolbar), 34

Q - R

T